MORE PASTA LIGHT

Eighty Delicious, Low-Fat Sauces

NORMAN KOLPAS
author of the bestselling *Pasta Light*

CONTEMPORARY
BOOKS
A TRIBUNE NEW MEDIA COMPANY

Library of Congress Cataloging-in-Publication Data

Norman, Norman.
    More pasta light : Eighty delicious, low-fat sauces / Norman
Kolpas.
        p.   cm.
    Sequel to: Pasta light.
    Includes Index.
    ISBN 0-8092-3725-3 (pbk. : alk. paper)
    1. Sauces.   2. Cookery (Pasta)   3. Low-fat diet—Recipes.
I. Title.
TX819.A1K6   1995
641.8'22—dc20   95-22525

For Katie and Jacob

Cover design by Laurie Liebewein
Cover photograph by Chris Cassidy
Foodstyling by Jenny Thornton

Featured on the cover: Sauté of Spring Vegetables with Fresh Herbs and Garlic

Published by Contemporary Books, Inc.
Two Prudential Plaza, Chicago, Illinois 60601-6790
Manufactured in the United States of America
International Standard Book Number: 0-8092-3725-3
10   9   8   7   6   5   4   3   2

Contents

Preface

More Pasta Light is much more than a simple sequel to *Pasta Light*. I wrote that previous book in response to a misconception that pasta was fattening, when in fact it is low in fat and an outstanding source of complex carbohydrates. The continuing success of *Pasta Light* attests to the revelation it has been for so many people.

That said, the public's knowledge of healthy eating has grown since I first started developing light pasta sauces. We know more all the time about what makes for a heart-healthy diet, and I've been wanting to apply some of the knowledge I've gained personally to a new collection of recipes that take even bolder strides toward a health-conscious way of eating.

The result is *More Pasta Light*. In this book, I have aimed to keep all recipes below the now widely accepted heart-healthy goal of deriving no more than 30 percent of our daily calories from fat. I've also tried to use more of the health-conscious ingredients being developed for the general consumer—better-quality fat-free cheeses, leaner meats, fat-free canned broths, and so on.

The result, I'm sure you'll see as you leaf through the recipes in this book, is a collection that achieves another goal of healthy eating today: that of enjoying a widely varied diet, one that is full of nutrients and is continually surprising and pleasing to the palate.

Acknowledgments

Many thanks to everyone at Contemporary Books, particularly Nancy Crossman, for her enthusiasm and support; Gerilee Hundt, for her patient shepherding of the manuscript; and Kim Bartko, Dana Draxten, Gigi Grajdura, Ellen Kollmon, Todd Petersen, Audrey Sails, Terry Stone, Alina Storek, and Kathy Willhoite.

Of all the friends and family members who partook of experiments in my kitchen, I'm especially indebted, as always, to my wife, Katie, and son, Jacob, for their love and good humor.

1

A Note on Dietary Information and Nutritional Analysis

Every recipe in this book includes a computer analysis of key aspects of its nutritional content per serving: calories, total fat, saturated fat, cholesterol, and sodium. You can use these figures as tools for incorporating the recipes into your own healthy eating plan. (All figures are based on a yield of four generous servings per recipe. If you'd like to serve smaller portions—six per recipe—multiply each nutritional analysis figure by two-thirds.)

If you want to figure the percentage of calories from fat, simply multiply the number of fat grams by nine (each gram of fat yields approximately nine calories); then divide that figure by the total number of calories and move the decimal point two places to the right. Thus, for example, a recipe with three grams of fat would get twenty-seven calories from fat. And if its total number of calories were, say, 203, the math would work out as: $27 \div 203 = .133$, or 13.3 percent of calories from fat.

Please bear in mind, however, that all these nutritional figures represent averages. No analysis will precisely match the dish as you yourself prepare it, because no two medium onions or cups of chicken broth or pounds of salmon or any other ingredients will be precisely identical or deliver precisely the same nutritional values.

Note also that in every recipe, I've directed you to season "to taste" with salt and pepper. For that reason, salt has not been figured into any of the nutritional analyses, and the figure given for "sodium" represents only the sodium content of the other ingredients in the recipe. In the past, anyone eating a heart-healthy diet tended to not add salt at all to his or her food, but recent studies have shown that only salt-sensitive individuals need be so wary, and you can feel free to season to taste with salt if your doctor says it's OK for you. (Remember that for every teaspoon of salt you add to any recipe in this book, you will increase the sodium content per serving by approximately 550 milligrams.)

One final, very important note: Please be sure to check with your doctor before embarking on any regimen that involves limiting your calories, fat, cholesterol, sodium, or any other dietary factors.

2
⁊

A Guide to Ingredients

Healthy ingredients are becoming more and more mainstream every day, and you should not have difficulty finding any of the ingredients I call for. I suggest you visit several local markets when you have a chance, and direct your business toward the one that offers you the best choices and the widest selections.

Let the following information on the ingredients I used and prepared for this book guide you in your own shopping.

Broths and Stocks

Many of these recipes gain intense flavor from "concentrated fat-free broth," prepared by boiling and reducing canned chicken broth.

Scan the soups section of your local market and you'll no doubt find a good selection of fat-free broths, with or without salt. I used Health Valley Chicken Broth, a fat-free and salt-free product with only 35 calories per cup; if you can't find it, contact Health Valley Foods, Inc., 16100 Foothill Blvd., Irwindale, CA 91706. Or substitute another commonly available brand. Swanson, for example, makes excellent fat-free, reduced-salt chicken and vegetable broths under its Natural Goodness label. Pritikin also markets good fat-free chicken and vegetable broths.

The best seafood stock I've found is the frozen product made and sold by Perfect Addition, P.O. Box 8976, Newport Beach, CA 92658; the company also makes frozen chicken, meat, and vegetable stocks.

To make concentrated, or condensed, broth: Put the broth in a heavy saucepan and boil over high heat until it reduces to half of its original volume— approximately 15 minutes. If you want to check along the way, stop once or twice and pour the broth into a heatproof measuring cup. If you plan to make several dishes calling for this ingredient in the next few days or weeks, you might want to prepare larger quantities. Store it in an airtight container in the refrigerator for several days or pack in freezer containers.

Butter Flavor Granules

Butter Buds brand of butter-flavored granules is a low-fat, cholesterol-free, low-sodium product that provides natural butter flavor. While you cannot sauté or fry with this product, you can reconstitute the granules to make a warm liquid convincingly resembling melted butter. You'll find I make use of this in several recipes in this book. If you can't find them, write to Cumberland Packing Corporation, Brooklyn, NY 11205.

Cheeses

Great strides are being made in creating reduced-fat and fat-free cheeses. Watch out for those products that are "reduced-fat" or "low-fat." Read their labels and you're likely to see calories derived from fat well in excess of 50 percent.

I was reluctant to recommend fat-free cheeses in the past because they lacked the melting qualities that came with butterfat content. But products from several companies now work well in pasta recipes. I've used and enjoyed those labeled Lifetime Fat Free, made by Lifeline Food Co., Inc., Seaside, CA 93955; and Alpine Lace of Maplewood, NJ 07040. I've also enjoyed the fluffy, creamy texture of fat-free ricotta cheese, sold in 15-ounce tubs under the Polly-O label from Pollio Dairy Products, Mineola, NY 11501; and the Frigo label from Frigo Cheese Corporation, Green Bay, WI 54307.

Cornstarch

The ground endosperm of the corn kernel, known as cornstarch—found in the baking section of any market—has the ability to quickly thicken a sauce to a rich, creamy consistency. I use it particularly in tandem with nonfat milk or evaporated skimmed milk to yield fat-free "cream" sauces.

Eggs

A few years ago, I was eagerly experimenting with cholesterol-free or fat-free egg substitutes, sold in the frozen-foods section of supermarkets. Frankly, they've always tasted a little flat or artificial to me. Lately, I've taken to using egg whites alone in recipes that call for eggs. I find that the palate gets used to the lack of yolk, and appreciates the fact that the egg still tastes natural.

Evaporated Skimmed Milk

I continue to add richness to pasta sauces by using canned evaporated skimmed milk, which is extremely low in butterfat yet rich in consistency and flavor. You'll find it in the baking section of your supermarket, along with low-fat and whole-milk versions, under the Carnation and Pet brand names.

Shallots and Garlic

These pungent ingredients pack a lot of flavor, adding great satisfaction to any pasta dish in which they appear.

Shallots, though less common than their two cousins, onions and garlic, are becoming increasingly available; they look like large individual garlic cloves with brown skins and purplish flesh, and you'll usually find them packaged in small net bags. They are as easy to pare and chop as an onion.

Garlic, with its tightly clinging, papery skin, presents the greatest challenge to the uninitiated. To pare a garlic clove, separate it from the bulb and press down on it firmly but carefully with the side of a broad-bladed knife. The skin then will easily slip off the slightly crushed clove.

Meat and Poultry

Nowadays, everyone knows about eating skinless white-meat chicken or turkey. Less well known is the fact that, thanks to newer breeding methods, which produce leaner animals, certain cuts of red meat can be virtually as low-fat as poultry. Pork tenderloin, for example, when trimmed of all visible fat and cooked, derives less than 28 percent of its calories from fat.

In many of the recipes in this book, I use healthier cuts of red meat to add heartiness to pasta dishes. Just trim away all visible fat before cooking.

Grinding your own meat and poultry: When a recipe calls for ground meat or poultry, the best way to ensure that you're getting a product as free of fat as possible is to buy the leanest cut you can find, trim it well, and grind it yourself. All you need to do the job is a food processor. Cut up the trimmed pork, lamb tenderloin, or skinless and boneless poultry breast meat into 1-inch cubes. Chill them in the freezer for about 1 hour. Then put the chunks in a food processor fitted with the metal blade and pulse until chopped to the desired degree.

Whenever you handle any raw meat or poultry, take extra care to avoid contamination by washing all utensils, work surfaces, and your hands thoroughly with soap and hot water.

Nuts

Though nuts are high in fat, just a sprinkling of them can go a long way to add rich taste and texture to dishes.

To toast nuts: Toasting develops the flavor and crispness of nuts. To toast nuts, spread them evenly on a foil-lined baking sheet in a 450°F oven. Toast until evenly light golden, 3 to 10 minutes depending on the size and type of the nuts. Carefully watch the nuts, because they can scorch quickly.

Peppers

To roast peppers: Both bell peppers and chili peppers develop intense, sweet flavor and tender texture when roasted. To roast them, place the peppers on a foil-lined baking sheet in a 500°F oven. Roast until evenly blistered and browned, 15 to 25 minutes depending on the size, turning the peppers several times to promote even roasting. Remove from the oven and cover with a kitchen towel until cool enough to handle.

Pull out the stems of the cooled peppers and peel away their blackened skins. Then open up the peppers and remove their seeds, using a small spoon to pick up any strays. Save the juices, which can add extra flavor to a sauce.

Cautionary note: When working with any hot chili peppers, take care not to touch your eyes or any other sensitive areas, and wear gloves if you have any cuts on your hands. Chilies contain fiery essential oils that can cause uncomfortable or painful burning sensations if precautions are not taken in their preparation.

Tomatoes

During the tomato's natural growing season in summer, keep an eye out for true vine-ripened tomatoes. At other times of year, you'll get the best fresh results from Roma tomatoes, also known in some areas as plum tomatoes.

For canned tomatoes, seek out a good brand available in your area, trying and tasting several different ones. While in previous books I have called for whole canned tomatoes, I find that many cooks haven't the desire or patience to crush them by hand when adding them to recipes; so in this book I simply call for canned crushed tomatoes. I used a brand to which salt had been added in the canning process, but if you're on a sodium-restricted diet, use tomatoes canned without added salt.

To peel fresh tomatoes: Bring a large saucepan of water to a boil. Use a small, sharp knife to cut out the core of each tomato and lightly score its skin into 4 segments. Use a slotted spoon or wire skimmer to carefully lower the tomato into the water and parboil it for 30 seconds or so; then transfer to a bowl filled with water and ice. When the tomatoes are cool enough to handle, peel their skins. To seed the tomatoes, cut each horizontally into halves and use your finger or the handle of a teaspoon to gently scoop out the seeds.

3

A Guide to Pasta

Several hundred different shapes and sizes of pasta have been cataloged by Italian culinary scholars. Though you'd have to scour Italy to find them all, you certainly can locate a score, or maybe dozens, of them in a well-stocked supermarket or Italian delicatessen.

Whatever the pasta's size or shape, the kind to seek out—and the type used throughout this book—is dried pasta made from durum-wheat semolina flour. You can, if you like, substitute fresh pasta; but keep in mind that it is likely to have been made with whole eggs, and while still well within the range of most healthy diets, it will be marginally higher in calories, fat, and cholesterol.

In each recipe's ingredients list, I suggest one or more types of pasta that will suit the preparation: delicate strands, for example, for a particularly elegant sauce; thick ribbons for a richer or creamier-textured topping; or fanciful, chewy shapes to accompany a particularly chunky or robust dish. Let my suggestions be just that—ideas to get you started—and feel free to substitute your own favorite type of pasta. The following broad categories and specific descriptions of commonly available pastas should help you to make your selection.

Strands

Angel hair. Extrafine strands. In Italian, *capelli d'angelo.*
Bavette. Slightly flattened spaghetti, oval in cross section.
Bucatini. Thin, spaghettilike strands with holes through the center.
Fedelini. Very thin spaghetti.
Fusilli. Thin, squiggly strands resembling fuses.
Perciatelli. Twice as thick as spaghetti, with a hole through its center like bucatini.
Spaghetti. Familiar stringlike pasta.
Vermicelli. Very thin spaghetti, resembling "little worms."

Ribbons

Fettuccelli. Narrower fettucine.
Fettucci. Half-inch-wide ribbons.
Fettuccine. Ribbons about ¼ inch wide.
Lasagne. Long ribbons 2 to 3 inches wide, usually layered with fillings and baked.
Linguine. Very narrow, thick ribbons resembling flattened spaghetti.
Mafalde. Wide ribbons with rippled edges.
Papardelle. Wide, short ribbons.
Tagliarini. Small, thin tagliatelle.
Tagliatelle. Similar to fettuccine, but somewhat wider.

Shapes

Bocconcini. Grooved tubes about 1½ inches long and ½ inch wide.
Bow ties. Resembling bow ties, usually about 2 inches wide. Sometimes called farfalle.
Cannolicchi. Small, ridged tubes.
Cavatelli. Narrow shells with rippled surfaces.

Conchiglie. Conch shells, varying in size and sometimes grooved.

Ditali. Short macaroni tubes.

Farfalle. "Butterflies." Similar to bow ties.

Gemelli. Two short strands intertwined like "twins."

Gnocchi. Small dumplinglike shapes.

Lumachi. Small snaillike shells.

Macaroni. Any pasta tube, but most commonly elbow macaroni—short, small to medium-sized curved tubes.

Maruzze. Shells, either smooth or ridged and varying in size from small to large.

Mostaccioli. "Little mustaches," 2 inches long, with diagonally cut ends, and sometimes grooved.

Penne. "Quill pens." Smooth or ridged short, narrow tubes with diagonally cut ends.

Radiatore. Small shapes resembling radiator grilles, about 1 inch square.

Rigatoni. Large grooved tubes.

Rotelli. Corkscrew spirals.

Ruote. Wagon wheels.

Ziti. Large macaronilike tubes cut into short or long lengths.

Cooking Pasta

Cooking times for pasta will vary depending on how thick and how dry any particular product is. For that reason, you should always refer to the manufacturer's suggested cooking time on the pasta packaging. Then follow these simple guidelines:

- Use a large quantity of water for the amount of pasta you are cooking, allowing plenty of room in the pot for the pasta to circulate freely.
- There is no need to add salt or oil to the water.

- Test a piece of pasta for doneness at the earliest possible time within the manufacturer's guidelines. Use a long fork or slotted spoon to remove a piece from the pot. Blow on it to cool it. Then bite into it. The pasta should be what the Italians call *al dente*—cooked through but still pleasantly chewy.

A Note on Cooking Times

All of the recipes in this book have been written to help you coordinate the simultaneous cooking of a sauce, the pasta, and sometimes other elements of the dish. But because the cooking time of any given pasta shape may vary by several minutes depending on its manufacturer, take note of the suggested cooking time and read through the recipe before starting to make sure that you understand how best to coordinate the dish so the pasta and its topping will be cooked and ready to serve at the same time.

Also, note that for every stage of a recipe, I try to give both a time range and some related sensory cue. Times will vary with the shape, size, and material of the cooking vessel you use, with the power of your stove, the weather, and all types of other factors. Please try to let your eyes, ears, nose, and taste buds guide you in the preparation of each recipe.

4

Vegetables

Peas and Shallots in White-Wine Broth

Moroccan Spiced Lentils and Vegetables

Broiled Vegetables and Garlic Broth

Three-Bean Chili

Corn with Fresh Chilies and Tomatoes

Broccoli with Black Olives, Capers, and Sun-Dried Tomatoes

Cauliflower and Cheese

Asparagus and Ham Sauté

Tangy Artichoke Sauce

Button Mushrooms with Roma Tomatoes and Fresh Herbs

Porcini with Tomatoes and Fresh Basil

Marinara with Capers and Lemon Zest

Fresh Tomatoes with Fines Herbes

Fresh Tomato-Basil Pesto

Vegetarian Spinach Lasagna

Tomatoes, Potatoes, and Rosemary

Kasha Varnishkas

Sauté of Spring Vegetables with Fresh Herbs and Garlic

Wilted Kale, White Beans, and Canadian Bacon

Mixed Vegetable Streamers

❧

Peas and Shallots in White-Wine Broth

This treatment for pasta is a real treat when fresh peas are in season.

> *1 cup dry white wine*
> *1½ cups condensed fat-free chicken broth (see page 4)*
> *1 pound fresh peas, shelled (about 1½ cups)*
> *4 medium shallots, very thinly sliced*
> *¾ pound dried small pasta shells*
> *Salt and pepper*
> *2 tablespoons finely chopped fresh Italian parsley*

In a small saucepan, bring the wine to a boil over moderate heat. Continue boiling until the wine is reduced by about a half, 7 to 10 minutes. While the wine reduces, bring a large pot of water to a boil.

Add the condensed chicken broth to the reduced wine and bring back to a boil. Add the peas and shallots and continue simmering until the peas are tender, about 5 minutes.

At the same time, add the pasta to the boiling water and cook until al dente. Drain the pasta and pour the wine broth and the peas and shallots on top. Season to taste with salt and pepper. Garnish with parsley.

Serves 4

NUTRITIONAL ANALYSIS PER SERVING
Calories: 399 *Total fat:* 1.57 g
Saturated fat: .23 g *Cholesterol:* 0 mg
Sodium: 70 mg

Moroccan Spiced Lentils and Vegetables

The ingredients and seasonings you might find in a Moroccan couscous join together in this rustic pasta dish. Feel free to substitute another type of lentil, or other vegetables of your choosing.

1 tablespoon vegetable oil
1 medium onion, coarsely chopped
2 medium garlic cloves, finely chopped
1 teaspoon hot paprika
1 teaspoon ground cumin
1 teaspoon whole caraway seeds
Pinch of cayenne pepper
1 16-ounce can crushed tomatoes
1 cup concentrated fat-free chicken broth (see page 4)
½ cup brown lentils
1 teaspoon sugar
1 medium carrot, cut into ½-inch dice
1 medium zucchini, cut into ½-inch dice
1 medium eggplant, left unpared, cut into ½-inch dice
¼ cup seedless golden or brown raisins
¾ pound dried farfalle or other medium-sized pasta shapes
Salt and pepper
1 tablespoon finely chopped fresh mint leaves

In a large skillet or saucepan, heat the vegetable oil with the onion and garlic over moderate heat. When they sizzle, add the paprika, cumin, caraway, and cayenne and sauté for about 1 minute more.

Add the tomatoes, concentrated chicken broth, lentils, and sugar and stir well. Simmer gently for about 15 minutes.

Meanwhile, bring a large pot of water to a boil.

Stir into the lentil mixture the carrot, zucchini, eggplant, and raisins. Continue simmering until the vegetables and lentils are tender and the sauce is thick, about 15 minutes more.

Add the pasta to the boiling water and cook until al dente, following manufacturer's suggested cooking time.

When the sauce is ready, season to taste with salt and pepper. Drain the pasta and immediately toss with the sauce. Garnish with mint.

Serves 4

NUTRITIONAL ANALYSIS PER SERVING
Calories: 570   *Total fat:* 5.8 g
Saturated fat: .75 g   *Cholesterol:* 0 mg
Sodium: 247 mg

Broiled Vegetables and Garlic Broth

Concentrated chicken broth, briefly simmered with garlic to add an extra dimension of flavor, forms the background for chunks of quickly grilled summer vegetables in this colorful presentation. Add other favorite summer squashes as you like.

4 small Roma tomatoes, cored and cut into ½-inch-thick slices
4 medium scallions, trimmed and left whole
4 large mushrooms, stemmed
2 medium zucchini, trimmed and cut lengthwise into halves
2 medium golden squash, trimmed and cut lengthwise into halves
2 medium Japanese eggplants, trimmed and cut lengthwise into halves
¼ cup lemon juice
2 tablespoons balsamic vinegar
Olive oil-flavored nonstick cooking spray
Salt and pepper
¾ pound dried farfalle, rotelli, or other medium-sized pasta shapes
1 cup concentrated fat-free chicken broth (see page 4)
2 medium garlic cloves, slightly crushed but left whole
2 tablespoons fat-free Parmesan cheese
2 tablespoons finely shredded fresh basil leaves

Remove the broiler tray and preheat the broiler. Bring a large pot of water to a boil.

In a large mixing bowl, toss the vegetables with the lemon juice and balsamic vinegar. Arrange the vegetables in a single layer on the broiler tray. Spray the vegetables evenly but lightly with nonstick cooking spray and season to taste with salt and pepper; turn the vegetables over and spray and season again.

Broil the vegetables close to the heat until golden brown, about 5 minutes per side. Turn them over and broil until golden, about 5 minutes more.

While the vegetables are broiling, add the pasta to the boiling water and cook until al dente, following manufacturer's suggested cooking time.

At the same time that the vegetables and pasta are cooking, in a small saucepan, heat the concentrated chicken broth with the garlic over low-to-moderate heat. When the broth begins to simmer, remove and discard the garlic.

Drain the pasta and immediately toss with the heated broth. Cut the vegetables into ½- to 1-inch pieces and scatter them on top. Garnish with Parmesan cheese and basil.

Serves 4

NUTRITIONAL ANALYSIS PER SERVING
Calories: 417   *Total fat:* 2.5 g
Saturated fat: .29 g   *Cholesterol:* 0 mg
Sodium: 110 mg

Three-Bean Chili

This vegetarian chili satisfies the taste buds with traditional Southwestern spice, while providing lots of beneficial dietary fiber.

1 tablespoon olive oil
1 medium onion, finely chopped
2 medium garlic cloves, finely chopped
1 long mild green chili pepper, stemmed and coarsely chopped
1 small hot green chili pepper, stemmed, seeded, and finely chopped
1 teaspoon mild pure red chili powder
1 teaspoon ground cumin
1 16-ounce can crushed tomatoes
¾ cup canned black beans, thoroughly rinsed and drained
¾ cup canned white beans, thoroughly rinsed and drained
½ cup canned garbanzo beans, thoroughly rinsed and drained
1 tablespoon tomato paste
1 tablespoon dried oregano
2 teaspoons sugar
1 bay leaf
¾ pound dried spaghetti or linguine
Salt and pepper
1 tablespoon finely chopped fresh cilantro leaves

In a large skillet or saucepan, heat the olive oil with the onion, garlic, and chili peppers over moderate-to-high heat. When they sizzle, sprinkle in the chili powder and cumin and sauté for 1 minute more.

Add the tomatoes, beans, tomato paste, oregano, sugar, and bay leaf. Simmer until the sauce is thick but still slightly liquid, about 15 minutes.

Meanwhile, bring a large pot of water to a boil. Add the pasta to the boiling water and cook until al dente, following manufacturer's suggested cooking time.

When the sauce is ready, remove and discard the bay leaf and season the sauce to taste with salt and pepper. Drain the pasta and toss gently with the sauce. Garnish with cilantro.

Serves 4

NUTRITIONAL ANALYSIS PER SERVING

Calories: 504	*Total fat:* 6.51 g
Saturated fat: .77 g	*Cholesterol:* 0 mg
Sodium: 468 mg	

Corn with Fresh Chilies and Tomatoes

When fresh sweet corn is in season, try making this with kernels stripped right from the cob. But if fresh corn is unavailable, don't let that stop you. This recipe is delicious with canned corn as well.

> *1 tablespoon olive oil*
> *1 small onion, finely chopped*
> *2 medium garlic cloves, finely chopped*
> *1 pound Roma or other firm, ripe tomatoes,*
>   *cored and coarsely chopped*
> *1 cup fresh corn kernels cut from the cob, or*
>   *1 cup drained canned corn kernels*
> *2 long green mild chili peppers, stemmed and cut into*
>   *¼-inch dice*
> *1 tablespoon finely chopped fresh basil leaves*
> *1 tablespoon finely chopped fresh oregano leaves*
> *1 teaspoon sugar*
> *¾ pound dried linguine or fettuccine*
> *Salt and pepper*
> *1 tablespoon finely chopped fresh cilantro or Italian parsley*

Bring a large pot of water to a boil.

In a large skillet, heat the olive oil over moderate heat. Add the onion and garlic and, as soon as they sizzle, stir in the tomatoes, corn, chili peppers, basil, oregano, and sugar. Sauté until the sauce thickens, about 10 minutes.

Meanwhile, add the pasta to the boiling water and cook until al dente, following manufacturer's suggested cooking time.

When the sauce is ready, season to taste with salt and pepper. Drain the pasta and immediately toss with the sauce. Garnish with cilantro or Italian parsley.

Serves 4

NUTRITIONAL ANALYSIS PER SERVING

Calories: 428   *Total fat:* 5.61 g
Saturated fat: .75 g   *Cholesterol:* 0 mg
Sodium: 24 mg

Broccoli with Black Olives, Capers, and Sun-Dried Tomatoes

If you like broccoli, there's no need to explain this sauce's appeal. If you're not a fan, however, you might be surprised by how nicely two kinds of tomatoes moderate the green vegetable's strong edge without disguising its distinctive character. This recipe is a study in intense flavors and colors. Black olives add another dimension, but because they're high in fat, use only a few.

½ tablespoon olive oil
2 medium shallots, finely chopped
2 medium garlic cloves, finely chopped
1 16-ounce can crushed tomatoes
½ cup dry white wine
1 tablespoon tomato paste
2 teaspoons sugar
1 teaspoon dried oregano
¼ teaspoon crushed red pepper flakes
¾ pound broccoli, tough stalks pared, stalks and florets
    coarsely chopped
1 dozen dry-packed sun-dried tomatoes, cut into
    ¼-inch-wide strips
1 dozen Mediterranean-style marinated black olives,
    rinsed and drained, pitted and cut into quarters

1 tablespoon drained small capers
¾ pound dried medium-sized shells, ruote, or other
*   similar-sized pasta shapes*
Salt and pepper

In a large nonstick saucepan, heat the olive oil, shallots, and garlic over moderate heat. As soon as they sizzle, add the canned tomatoes, wine, tomato paste, sugar, oregano, and red pepper flakes.

Bring the mixture to a boil, stirring, and add the broccoli, sun-dried tomatoes, olives, and capers. Reduce the heat and simmer until the broccoli is tender and the sauce is thick but still slightly liquid, about 15 minutes.

Meanwhile, bring a large pot of water to a boil. Add the pasta and cook until al dente, following manufacturer's suggested cooking time.

When the sauce is ready, season to taste with salt and pepper. Drain the pasta and immediately toss with the sauce.

Serves 4

NUTRITIONAL ANALYSIS PER SERVING
Calories: 456   *Total fat:* 6.38 g
Saturated fat: .78 g   *Cholesterol:* 0 mg
Sodium: 542 mg

Cauliflower and Cheese

A favorite childhood treatment for cauliflower becomes a healthy pasta topping with the help of evaporated skimmed milk and fat-free cheese. If you like, try adding some slivers of lean Canadian bacon, heating them with the sauce for a minute or two before serving.

¾ pound cauliflower, cut into ½- to 1-inch pieces
1 12-ounce can evaporated skimmed milk
1 tablespoon cornstarch
¾ pound dried medium-sized elbow macaroni, shells,
    or other pasta shapes
¼ pound fat-free cheddar cheese, thinly shredded
¼ pound fat-free Swiss cheese, thinly shredded
Salt and white pepper
1 tablespoon finely chopped fresh Italian parsley
1 tablespoon finely chopped fresh chives

Bring a medium saucepan of water to a boil. Add the cauliflower, bring back to a full boil, drain well, and set aside. Rinse out the saucepan.

Pour ½ cup of the evaporated milk into a small bowl or cup. Sprinkle in the cornstarch and stir until dissolved. Set aside.

Bring a large pot of water to a boil. Add the pasta and cook until al dente, following manufacturer's suggested cooking time.

Meanwhile, in the medium saucepan, bring the remaining evaporated milk to a boil over moderate heat. Add the cauliflower, reduce the heat, and cook until tender, 5 to 7 minutes.

Stir in the cheeses. When the cheeses begin to melt, briefly stir the cornstarch-milk mixture and pour it into the pan. Continue simmering and stirring until the sauce thickens. Season to taste with salt and white pepper.

Drain the pasta and immediately toss with the sauce. Garnish with parsley and chives.

Serves 4

Nutritional analysis per serving

Calories: 499	*Total fat:* 1.68 g
Saturated fat: .32 g	*Cholesterol:* 9 mg
Sodium: 550 mg	

Asparagus and Ham Sauté

Nothing complements the flavor of fresh springtime asparagus quite like the smoky taste of ham. Being fairly lean, the ham doesn't really detract from the healthiness of the dish; if you're concerned about the ham's salt content, seek out one of the low-salt varieties of ham available in well-stocked delicatessens.

¾ pound dried spaghettini, spaghetti, or other thin
    pasta strands
1 tablespoon olive oil
2 medium shallots, finely chopped
1 pound asparagus, trimmed and cut diagonally into
    ¼-inch-thick slices
¼ pound lean smoked ham or Canadian bacon,
    very thinly sliced and cut into ¼ by 1-inch strips
1 cup concentrated nonfat chicken broth (see page 4)
Salt and pepper
1 tablespoon finely chopped fresh Italian parsley
1 tablespoon finely chopped fresh chives

Bring a large pot of water to a boil. Add the pasta and cook until al dente, following manufacturer's suggested cooking time.

Meanwhile, in a large nonstick skillet, heat the olive oil and shallots over moderate-to-high heat. As soon as the shallots sizzle, add the asparagus and ham and sauté about 2 minutes. Add the concentrated broth, raise the heat to high and continue cooking until the broth is hot and the asparagus is tender-crisp, about 1 minute more. Season to taste with salt and pepper.

Drain the pasta and immediately toss with the sauce. Garnish with parsley and chives.

Serves 4

NUTRITIONAL ANALYSIS PER SERVING
Calories: 423   *Total fat:* 6.29 g
Saturated fat: 1.13 g   *Cholesterol:* 13 mg
Sodium: 452 mg

༄

Tangy Artichoke Sauce

For a quick, healthy pasta meal featuring artichokes, there's no need to go through tedious preparation of the prickly thistle. Just head for the canned vegetable section of your market and pick up some water-packed artichoke hearts to use in this simple sauce.

½ tablespoon olive oil
2 medium shallots, finely chopped
2 medium garlic cloves, finely chopped
1 16-ounce can crushed tomatoes
1 14-ounce can water-packed artichoke hearts, drained,
    each heart cut into quarters
1 tablespoon tomato paste
1 tablespoon drained small capers
2 teaspoons sugar
1 teaspoon balsamic vinegar
2 teaspoons dried marjoram
1 teaspoon dried oregano
1 teaspoon dried thyme
1 bay leaf
¾ pound dried farfalle or other medium-sized pasta shapes
2 teaspoons grated lemon zest
Salt and pepper
2 tablespoons finely chopped fresh Italian parsley

Bring a large pot of water to a boil.

Meanwhile, in a large nonstick skillet or saucepan, heat the olive oil with the shallots and garlic over moderate heat. When they sizzle, add the tomatoes, artichoke hearts, tomato paste, capers, sugar, balsamic vinegar, marjoram, oregano, thyme, and bay leaf. Simmer briskly, stirring occasionally, until the sauce is thick but still slightly liquid, 10 to 15 minutes.

While the sauce cooks, add the pasta to the boiling water and cook until al dente, following manufacturer's suggested cooking time.

Remove and discard the bay leaf from the sauce. Stir in the lemon zest and season to taste with salt and pepper.

Drain the pasta and immediately toss with the sauce. Garnish with parsley.

Serves 4

NUTRITIONAL ANALYSIS PER SERVING
Calories: 398   *Total fat:* 3.40 g
Saturated fat: .45 g   *Cholesterol:* 0 mg
Sodium: 280 mg

❧

Button Mushrooms with Roma Tomatoes and Fresh Herbs

The charm of this dish relies on finding the smallest button mushrooms available, no more than an inch wide if possible; so take a little time to sort through the supermarket bin. Try varying the mixture of fresh herbs to suit your fancy.

> *1 tablespoon olive oil*
> *4 medium shallots, finely chopped*
> *¾ pound small button mushrooms, trimmed but left whole*
> *1 pound Roma or other firm, ripe tomatoes, cored, halved,*
> *   seeded (see page 8), and coarsely chopped*
> *1 tablespoon finely chopped fresh Italian parsley*
> *1 tablespoon finely chopped fresh basil leaves*
> *2 teaspoons finely chopped fresh tarragon leaves*
> *¾ pound dried linguine or fettuccine*
> *Salt and pepper*

Bring a large pot of water to a boil.

Meanwhile, in a large nonstick skillet, heat the olive oil and shallots over moderate heat. When the shallots sizzle, add the mushrooms and sauté about 1 minute.

Add the tomatoes and herbs and continue cooking until the tomato juices thicken, 7 to 10 minutes.

Meanwhile, add the pasta to the boiling water and cook until al dente, following manufacturer's suggested cooking time.

When the sauce is ready, season to taste with salt and pepper. Drain the pasta and immediately toss with the sauce.

Serves 4

NUTRITIONAL ANALYSIS PER SERVING
Calories: 396   *Total fat:* 5.41 g
Saturated fat: .73 g   *Cholesterol:* 0 mg
Sodium: 20 mg

Porcini with Tomatoes and Fresh Basil

Dried porcini mushrooms, available in well-stocked food stores and Italian delicatessens, add a rich meaty savor to this tomato-based sauce.

> *2 ounces dried porcini mushrooms*
> *½ cup dry red wine*
> *½ tablespoon olive oil*
> *4 medium shallots, finely chopped*
> *2 medium garlic cloves, finely chopped*
> *1 16-ounce can crushed tomatoes*
> *1 tablespoon tomato paste*
> *2 teaspoons sugar*
> *1 bay leaf*
> *¾ pound dried spaghetti or linguine*
> *Salt and pepper*
> *⅓ cup packed finely shredded fresh basil leaves*

Put the porcini in a small bowl and add the wine. Let soak until soft, about 10 minutes.

Meanwhile, bring a large pot of water to a boil.

Remove the porcini from the wine and finely chop. Pour the wine through a small wire strainer lined with cheesecloth and held over a cup or bowl. Reserve the wine.

In a large skillet or saucepan, heat the olive oil with the shallots and garlic over moderate heat. When they sizzle, add the chopped porcini and sauté about 1 minute more.

Add the reserved wine, the tomatoes, tomato paste, sugar, and bay leaf. Simmer briskly until the sauce is thick but still slightly liquid, 10 to 15 minutes.

While the sauce simmers, add the pasta to the boiling water and cook until al dente, following manufacturer's suggested cooking time.

When the sauce is ready, remove and discard the bay leaf. Season the sauce to taste with salt and pepper and stir in the basil. Drain the pasta and immediately toss with the sauce.

Serves 4

NUTRITIONAL ANALYSIS PER SERVING
Calories: 442   *Total fat:* 3.67 g
Saturated fat: .45 g   *Cholesterol:* 0 mg
Sodium: 232 mg

ॐ

Marinara with Capers and Lemon Zest

Whole little capers and shredded lemon zest give a lively lift to a simple tomato sauce. If you'd really like to dress up this dish, throw in a handful of precooked bay shrimp just before serving.

> ½ tablespoon olive oil
> 2 medium shallots, finely chopped
> 2 medium garlic cloves, finely chopped
> 1 28-ounce can crushed tomatoes
> 2 tablespoons small capers, rinsed and drained
> 2 tablespoons finely chopped fresh basil leaves
> 2 tablespoons finely chopped fresh Italian parsley
> 1 tablespoon tomato paste
> 1 tablespoon sugar
> 1 teaspoon dried oregano
> 2 bay leaves
> ¾ pound dried angel hair or spaghettini
> 1 tablespoon grated lemon zest
> Salt and pepper

Bring a large pot of water to a boil.

Meanwhile, in a medium nonstick skillet or saucepan, heat the olive oil with the shallots and garlic over moderate heat. When they sizzle, add the tomatoes, capers, basil, parsley, tomato paste, sugar, oregano, and bay leaves. Raise the heat slightly and simmer until the sauce is thick but still fairly liquid, about 15 minutes.

While the sauce is cooking, add the pasta to the boiling water and cook until al dente, following manufacturer's suggested cooking time.

When the sauce is ready, remove and discard the bay leaves. Stir in the lemon zest and season to taste with salt and pepper. Drain the pasta and immediately toss with the sauce.

Serves 4

NUTRITIONAL ANALYSIS PER SERVING
Calories: 397   *Total fat:* 3.61 g
Saturated fat: .49 g *Cholesterol:* 0 mg
Sodium: 474 mg

Fresh Tomatoes with Fines Herbes

The fines herbes of the classic French kitchen add extra finesse to a sauce showing off the flavor of vine-ripened summer tomatoes.

> *½ tablespoon olive oil*
> *2 medium shallots, finely chopped*
> *1½ pounds firm, vine-ripened summer tomatoes, cored,*
> *   halved, seeded (see page 8), and coarsely chopped*
> *2 tablespoons finely chopped fresh Italian parsley*
> *2 tablespoons finely chopped fresh basil leaves*
> *1 tablespoon finely chopped fresh chervil*
> *2 teaspoons finely chopped fresh dillweed*
> *1 teaspoon finely chopped fresh tarragon leaves*
> *¾ pound dried angel hair, spaghettini, or spaghetti*
> *Salt and pepper*

Bring a large pot of water to a boil.

Meanwhile, in a large nonstick skillet, heat the olive oil and shallots over moderate heat. When the shallots sizzle, stir in the tomatoes and herbs. Sauté just until the tomato juices thicken, 7 to 10 minutes.

As soon as the tomatoes start cooking, add the pasta to the boiling water and cook until al dente, following manufacturer's suggested cooking time.

When the sauce is ready, season to taste with salt and pepper. Drain the pasta and immediately toss with the sauce.

Serves 4

NUTRITIONAL ANALYSIS PER SERVING
Calories: 370   *Total fat:* 3.55 g
Saturated fat: .48 g   *Cholesterol:* 0 mg
Sodium: 22 mg

❧

Fresh Tomato-Basil Pesto

Classic basil pesto gets some of its rich flavor and body from pine nuts, Parmesan cheese, and olive oil, all of which are high in fat. In this variation, though, tomatoes provide some of that body and add a new dimension of flavor—without entirely forsaking the nuts, cheese, or oil.

¾ pound dried spaghetti, linguine, or fettuccine
3 cups packed stemmed fresh basil leaves
4 medium Roma tomatoes, cored, peeled (see page 8),
   and coarsely chopped
⅓ to ½ cup concentrated fat-free chicken broth (see page 4)
2 tablespoons grated nonfat Parmesan cheese
2 tablespoons toasted pine nuts (see page 7)
2 tablespoons olive oil
2 medium garlic cloves
Salt and pepper

Bring a large pot of water to a boil. Add the pasta and cook until al dente, following manufacturer's suggested cooking time.

Meanwhile, put the basil, tomatoes, ⅓ cup of the concentrated broth, the Parmesan cheese, pine nuts, olive oil, and garlic in a food processor fitted with the metal blade. Pulse the ingredients until they are coarsely chopped, then scrape down the work bowl and process until the mixture is smoothly pureed, adding more of the broth if necessary to achieve a thick but slightly fluid consistency. Season to taste with salt and pepper.

As soon as the pasta is cooked, drain it and immediately toss with the pesto.

Serves 4

NUTRITIONAL ANALYSIS PER SERVING
Calories: 473   *Total fat:* 11.21 g
Saturated fat: 1.47 g   *Cholesterol:* 0 mg
Sodium: 80 mg

Vegetarian Spinach Lasagna

This variation on lasagna highlights the natural affinity between spinach and garlic.

⅓ pound dried lasagna noodles
1 tablespoon olive oil
4 medium garlic cloves, finely chopped
2 bunches spinach, stemmed, ribbed, and thoroughly washed,
*   leaves cut crosswise into ¼-inch-wide strips*
½ cup condensed fat-free vegetable broth (see page 4)
Salt and pepper
15 ounces fat-free ricotta cheese
¼ cup grated Romano cheese
2 tablespoons finely shredded fresh basil leaves
2 tablespoons finely chopped fresh Italian parsley
2 egg whites, lightly beaten
Nonstick cooking spray
½ pound fat-free mozzarella or Monterey Jack cheese,
*   coarsely shredded*

Bring a large pot of water to a boil. Add the pasta and cook until al dente, following manufacturer's suggested cooking time. Drain.

Meanwhile, in a large nonstick skillet or saucepan, heat the olive oil with the garlic over moderate heat. When the garlic sizzles, add the spinach and sauté until the spinach begins to wilt, about 30 seconds. Add the condensed vegetable broth and continue sautéing until the spinach is completely wilted and tender, 1 to 2 minutes more. Season to taste with salt and pepper and set aside.

In a mixing bowl, stir together the ricotta and Romano cheeses, basil, parsley, and egg whites. Season to taste with salt and pepper.

Preheat the oven to 375°F.

Lightly spray a deep 8-inch-square baking dish with nonstick cooking spray. Lightly spoon a little of the liquid from the spinach on the bottom of the dish. Arrange one-third of the cooked pasta on top, trimming the noodles to fit. Spread one-third of the spinach on the noodles, then a third of the ricotta mixture, and a third of the mozzarella. Repeat in that order until all the ingredients are used, ending with the mozzarella.

Cover the dish loosely with foil, not touching the mozzarella, and bake for about 30 minutes. Remove the foil and bake 20 to 30 minutes more, until the lasagna is bubbly and the top is golden. Remove from the oven and let the lasagna settle for 5 to 10 minutes before slicing and serving.

Serves 4

NUTRITIONAL ANALYSIS PER SERVING
Calories: 411   *Total fat:* 6.00 g
Saturated fat: .60 g   *Cholesterol:* 15 mg
Sodium: 863 mg

❧

Tomatoes, Potatoes, and Rosemary

Inspired by rustic Italian cookery, this robust vegetarian pasta dish satisfies with chunks of potato and the fragrance of fresh rosemary. In an interesting twist on sauce preparation, the potatoes actually cook with the pasta.

2 medium baking potatoes, pared and cut into ½-inch cubes
1 tablespoon olive oil
1 small onion, finely chopped
2 medium garlic cloves, finely chopped
1 16-ounce can crushed tomatoes
1 tablespoon tomato paste
2 teaspoons finely chopped fresh rosemary leaves
2 teaspoons sugar
¾ pound dried farfalle or fusilli
Salt and pepper

Bring a large pot of water to a boil and add the potato cubes.

Meanwhile, in a large nonstick skillet or saucepan, heat the olive oil with the onion and garlic over moderate heat. As soon as they sizzle, stir in the tomatoes, tomato paste, rosemary, and sugar. Simmer until the sauce is thick but still slightly liquid, 10 to 15 minutes.

Add the pasta to the potatoes in the boiling water and cook until al dente, following manufacturer's suggested cooking time, and the potatoes are tender.

When the sauce is ready, season to taste with salt and pepper. Drain the pasta and potatoes and immediately toss with the sauce.

Serves 4

NUTRITIONAL ANALYSIS PER SERVING
Calories: 444   *Total fat:* 5.13 g
Saturated fat: .69 g   *Cholesterol:* 0 mg
Sodium: 228 mg

❧
Kasha Varnishkas

If you enjoy the earthy, sour flavor of buckwheat, you'll love this traditional Russian mixture of buckwheat groats (kasha) and pasta, which makes a satisfyingly rustic luncheon or dinner dish. I add a little liquified Butter Buds to moisten it just before serving.

> 1 cup buckwheat groats
> 3 cups fat-free chicken broth
> ¾ pound dried farfalle or bow-tie pasta
> 1 tablespoon vegetable oil
> 1 medium onion, finely chopped
> 1 packet (½ ounce) Butter Buds brand natural butter
>   flavoring
> ½ cup hot tap water
> 2 tablespoons finely chopped fresh Italian parsley
> 2 tablespoons finely chopped fresh chives
> Salt and pepper

In a nonstick saucepan, cook the buckwheat groats over moderate heat, stirring frequently, until they are lightly browned and give off a toasty, slightly sour aroma, 7 to 10 minutes.

Add the chicken broth, bring to a boil, and reduce the heat to very low. Cover the pan and simmer gently until the groats have absorbed all the liquid and are tender, 20 to 30 minutes. If the groats seem dry before they are fully cooked, add a little boiling water.

Meanwhile, bring a large pot of water to a boil. Add the pasta and cook until al dente, following manufacturer's suggested cooking time.

While the pasta and buckwheat are cooking, in a medium nonstick skillet, heat the vegetable oil over moderate heat. Add the onion and sauté until golden brown, 5 to 7 minutes. Set aside.

In a measuring cup or bowl, stir the Butter Buds into the ½ cup of hot water until completely dissolved. Set aside.

As soon as the pasta is cooked, drain well and add along with the kasha to the skillet with the onions. Drizzle in the liquified Butter Buds, add the parsley and chives and toss well. Season to taste with salt and pepper.

Serves 4

NUTRITIONAL ANALYSIS PER SERVING
Calories: 543   *Total fat:* 5.91 g
Saturated fat: .87 g   *Cholesterol:* .70 mg
Sodium: 239 mg

೫

Sauté of Spring Vegetables with Fresh Herbs and Garlic

Nothing compares to how the color, texture, or flavor of fresh springtime vegetables—especially the year's first asparagus—can please the appetite in the healthiest of ways. Add your own favorite spring vegetables, cut up into quick-cooking pieces, to this medley.

¾ pound dried fettuccine or tagliatelle
1 tablespoon olive oil
4 medium garlic cloves, finely chopped
1 pound slender asparagus, trimmed and cut into 2-inch pieces
½ pound small cultivated mushrooms, trimmed and cut into
    ¼-inch-thick slices
½ pound firm ripe cherry tomatoes, stemmed and cut into quarters
¾ cup concentrated fat-free vegetable broth (see page 4)
Salt and white pepper
1 tablespoon finely chopped fresh basil leaves
1 tablespoon finely chopped fresh Italian parsley
½ tablespoon finely chopped fresh oregano leaves

Bring a large pot of water to a boil. Add the pasta and cook until al dente, following manufacturer's suggested cooking time.

About halfway through the pasta's cooking time, in a large nonstick skillet, heat the olive oil and garlic over moderate heat. When the garlic sizzles, add the asparagus, mushrooms, and tomatoes, raise the heat to high and sauté until the asparagus turns bright green, about 3 minutes.

Add the concentrated vegetable broth, bring to a boil, and simmer briskly until the asparagus is al dente, 2 to 3 minutes more. Season to taste with salt and white pepper.

Drain the pasta and immediately toss with the vegetables and broth and the basil, parsley, and oregano.

Serves 4

NUTRITIONAL ANALYSIS PER SERVING
Calories: 408   *Total fat:* 5.37 g
Saturated fat: .74 g   *Cholesterol:* 0 mg
Sodium: 110 mg

Wilted Kale, White Beans, and Canadian Bacon

Cooked kale has a robust flavor that goes very well with pasta and contrasts wonderfully with the earthy taste and smooth texture of white beans. The smoky hint of Canadian bacon complements both the kale and the beans, giving them a down-home quality that is very satisfying. If you like (and don't mind adding some calories and fat), sprinkle with Parmesan or Romano cheese at table.

¾ pound dried farfalle, ruote, or other medium-sized to large
    pasta shapes
½ tablespoon olive oil
2 medium garlic cloves, finely chopped
1 pound fresh kale, stems and ribs trimmed and discarded,
    leaves cut crosswise into ½-inch-wide strips
¼ pound Canadian bacon, trimmed and cut into
    ¼- by 1-inch strips
2 cups concentrated fat-free chicken broth (see page 4)
1 cup canned white beans, rinsed and drained
Salt and pepper

Bring a large pot of water to a boil. Add the pasta and cook until al dente, following manufacturer's suggested cooking time.

In a large nonstick skillet, heat the olive oil and garlic over moderate heat. As soon as the garlic sizzles, add the kale and Canadian bacon and sauté about 1 minute, stirring to coat the leaves evenly with the garlic and oil and to wilt them slightly.

Add the concentrated chicken broth and the beans, raise the heat to high, and bring to a boil. Reduce the heat and simmer briskly until the kale is tender-crisp, 5 to 7 minutes more.

Drain the pasta and immediately toss with the broth, kale, beans, and Canadian bacon. Season to taste with salt and pepper.

Serves 4

NUTRITIONAL ANALYSIS PER SERVING
Calories: 492   *Total fat:* 5.82 g
Saturated fat: 1.12 g   *Cholesterol:* 14 mg
Sodium: 641 mg

Mixed Vegetable Streamers

Thin, al dente shreds of a variety of vegetables give this rapid preparation a kaleidoscope of colors, tastes, and textures. Use the shredding disc on your food processor, if you like, placing lengths of the vegetables horizontally in the feed tube to get the longest strips possible. If you don't require a strictly vegetarian version, you can substitute concentrated chicken broth for the concentrated vegetable broth.

¾ pound dried spaghetti or linguine
½ tablespoon olive oil
2 medium shallots, finely chopped
1 medium carrot, pared and cut into long, thin shreds with a
    handheld grater or food processor
1 medium parsnip, pared and cut into long, thin shreds with a
    handheld grater or food processor
1 medium red bell pepper, halved, stemmed, seeded, and cut into
    long, thin shreds with a handheld grater or food processor
½ pound broccoli stems, pared and cut into long, thin shreds with a
    handheld grater or food processor
1½ cups concentrated fat-free vegetable broth (see page 4)
Salt and pepper
2 tablespoons finely chopped fresh Italian parsley

Bring a large pot of water to a boil. Add the pasta and cook until al dente, following manufacturer's suggested cooking time.

Meanwhile, in a large nonstick skillet, heat the olive oil and shallots over moderate heat. As soon as the shallots sizzle, add the vegetables and sauté, stirring constantly, for about 1 minute, until they are well mixed. Add the concentrated vegetable broth, bring to a boil, and cook until the vegetables are tender-crisp, 2 to 3 minutes more. Season to taste with salt and pepper.

Drain the pasta and immediately toss with the vegetables and broth. Garnish with parsley.

Serves 4

NUTRITIONAL ANALYSIS PER SERVING
Calories: 405   *Total fat:* 3.46 g
Saturated fat: .42 g   *Cholesterol:* 0 mg
Sodium: 216 mg

5

Seafood

Salmon Caviar with Lemon Butter

Grilled Salmon with Miso Broth

Grilled Salmon with Yellow Bell Pepper Pesto

Smoked Salmon with Red Onion, Capers, and Chives

Chunky Ahi Tuna with Arugula and Radicchio

Tuna with Tomato and Fresh Dillweed

Grilled Cajun Swordfish with Chili Broth

Lemon-Dill Shrimp with Vodka Broth

Chili-Rubbed Shrimp with Santa Fe Tomato Sauce

Sautéed Shrimp with Roasted Red Bell Peppers

Seared Sea Scallops in Shallot Broth with Chives

Grilled Scallops with Roasted Red Pepper Pesto

Steamed Clams in Roasted Garlic Broth

Clams Arrabiata

Creamy White-Wine Clam Sauce

Mussels with Lemon Zest–Tomato Broth

Seafood Celebration

❧

Salmon Caviar with Lemon Butter

Elegance and lightness combine in this very simple presentation that highlights the sublime flavor of salmon eggs, which are available in jars in most quality markets or gourmet food shops.

> *¾ pound dried angel hair or spaghettini*
> *1 packet (½ ounce) Butter Buds brand natural butter flavoring*
> *½ cup hot tap water*
> *2 teaspoons lemon juice*
> *2 teaspoons grated lemon zest*
> *6 tablespoons salmon roe*
> *2 tablespoons finely chopped fresh chives*
> *Black pepper*

Bring a large pot of water to a boil. Add the pasta and cook until al dente.

Meanwhile, in a measuring cup or bowl, stir the Butter Buds into the ½ cup of hot water until completely dissolved. Set aside.

As soon as the pasta is cooked, drain it and immediately toss it with the liquified Butter Buds, the lemon juice, and lemon zest. Scatter the salmon roe and chives on top and season generously to taste with black pepper.

Serves 4

NUTRITIONAL ANALYSIS PER SERVING
Calories: 389   *Total fat:* 4.07 g
Saturated fat: .81 g   *Cholesterol:* 160 mg
Sodium: 177 mg

❧

Grilled Salmon with Miso Broth

In this Asian-style presentation, salmon fillets and the broth that accompanies them gain rich flavor, without a lot of fat, from Japanese soybean paste. You could, if you wish, substitute concentrated fat-free chicken broth (see page 4) for the fish stock.

> *6 tablespoons Japanese yellow miso (soybean paste)*
> *2 tablespoons light soy sauce*
> *1 tablespoon mirin (Japanese rice wine)*
> *1 tablespoon finely grated fresh gingerroot*
> *1 pound fresh salmon fillet, cut into*
>   *½-inch-thick medallions*
> *¾ pound dried angel hair or spaghettini*
> *2 cups rich salt-free fish stock*
> *2 tablespoons finely chopped fresh chives*

In a wide, shallow dish, stir together 4 tablespoons of the miso with the soy sauce, mirin, and gingerroot. Add the salmon medallions and turn them in the mixture to coat evenly. Marinate at room temperature for about 15 minutes.

Meanwhile, bring a large pot of water to a boil and preheat the broiler or grill until very hot.

Remove the salmon medallions from the marinade. Broil or grill close to the heat until nicely browned, 4 to 5 minutes per side.

While the salmon is cooking, cook the pasta until al dente, following manufacturer's suggested cooking time. Also at the same time, in a medium saucepan, heat the fish stock over moderate heat and stir in the remaining miso.

Drain the pasta and divide it among individual shallow serving bowls. Ladle the miso broth over the pasta. Place the salmon medallions on top and garnish with chives.

Serves 4

NUTRITIONAL ANALYSIS PER SERVING
Calories: 522   *Total fat:* 9.31 g
Saturated fat: 1.41 g   *Cholesterol:* 62 mg
Sodium: 746 mg

Grilled Salmon with Yellow Bell Pepper Pesto

Try this recipe for an elegant dinner party. The vivid pink salmon looks so beautiful against a thick sauce made from roasted yellow bell peppers, which are commonly available now in well-stocked supermarkets and produce stores.

½ cup lemon juice
1 pound fresh salmon fillet, cut into ½-inch-thick medallions
Olive oil-flavored nonstick cooking spray
Salt and white pepper
¾ pound dried angel hair or spaghettini
4 medium yellow bell peppers, roasted, stemmed, peeled,
    and seeded (see page 7), juices saved
¼ cup rich salt-free fish stock
2 tablespoons grated Romano cheese
1 tablespoon olive oil
2 tablespoons finely chopped fresh chives
1 tablespoon finely chopped fresh Italian parsley

In a wide, shallow dish, pour half of the lemon juice. Add the salmon medallions and turn them in the juice to coat evenly. Marinate at room temperature for about 15 minutes.

Meanwhile, bring a large pot of water to a boil and preheat the broiler or grill until very hot.

Remove the salmon medallions from the lemon juice. Spray them lightly but evenly with the nonstick spray and season to taste with salt and white pepper. Broil or grill close to the heat until nicely browned, 4 to 5 minutes per side.

While the salmon is cooking, cook the pasta until al dente, following manufacturer's suggested cooking time.

Also at the same time, put the peppers and their juices, the remaining lemon juice, half of the fish stock, the Romano cheese, and olive oil in a food processor fitted with the metal blade. Pulse the ingredients until they are coarsely chopped, then scrape down the work bowl and process until the mixture is smoothly pureed, adding more of the fish stock if necessary to achieve a thick but slightly fluid consistency. Season to taste with salt and white pepper.

Drain the pasta and divide it among individual shallow serving bowls. Spoon the pesto over the pasta. Place the salmon medallions on top. Garnish with chives and parsley.

Serves 4

NUTRITIONAL ANALYSIS PER SERVING
Calories: 547   *Total fat:* 13.04 g
Saturated fat: 1.78 g   *Cholesterol:* 65 mg
Sodium: 103 mg

Smoked Salmon with Red Onion, Capers, and Chives

Here pasta receives a sophisticated deli-style treatment, complemented by a hint of lemon and the rich flavor of liquified Butter Buds. For the best flavor and less fat, however, buy good-quality Scotch-style smoked salmon rather than delicatessen lox.

¾ pound dried angel hair, spaghettini, or spaghetti
1 packet (½ ounce) Butter Buds brand natural
  butter flavoring
½ cup hot tap water
6 ounces thinly sliced smoked salmon, cut crosswise
  into ¼-inch-wide strips
½ small red onion, finely chopped
1 tablespoon small capers, rinsed and drained
2 teaspoons lemon juice
2 teaspoons grated lemon zest
Black pepper
1 tablespoon finely chopped fresh chives

Bring a large pot of water to a boil. Add the pasta and cook until al dente, following manufacturer's suggested cooking time.

Meanwhile, in a measuring cup or bowl, stir the Butter Buds into the ½ cup of hot water until completely dissolved. Set aside.

As soon as the pasta is cooked, drain it and immediately toss with the liquified Butter Buds, the smoked salmon, onion, capers, lemon juice, and lemon zest. Season generously to taste with black pepper and garnish with chives.

Serves 4

NUTRITIONAL ANALYSIS PER SERVING
Calories: 385   *Total fat:* 3.18 g
Saturated fat: 3.18 g   *Cholesterol:* 10 mg
Sodium: 567 mg

Chunky Ahi Tuna with Arugula and Radicchio

If you've never tried arugula or radicchio, you'll be surprised by how well these two slightly bitter salad greens—both of which are becoming widely available in well-stocked produce shops or supermarkets—will complement the taste of fresh grilled tuna served atop a quickly prepared tomato sauce.

1 tablespoon lemon juice
1 tablespoon balsamic vinegar
1 tablespoon olive oil
¾ pound fresh ahi tuna fillet
2 medium heads radicchio, cut lengthwise into halves
1 small onion, finely chopped
1 medium garlic clove, finely chopped
1 16-ounce can crushed tomatoes
½ cup rich salt-free fish stock
1 tablespoon tomato paste
2 teaspoons sugar
½ tablespoon dried marjoram
½ tablespoon dried oregano
1 bay leaf
Salt and pepper
¾ pound dried spaghetti or linguine
¾ cup packed whole arugula leaves
2 tablespoons finely shredded fresh basil leaves

In a large, shallow dish, stir together the lemon juice, balsamic vinegar, and ½ tablespoon of the olive oil. Add the tuna and radicchio and turn them in the mixture to coat evenly. Marinate at room temperature about 30 minutes. Meanwhile, preheat the broiler or grill until very hot.

After about 15 minutes of marinating, in a large nonstick skillet or saucepan, heat the remaining olive oil with the onion and garlic over moderate heat. When they sizzle, add the tomatoes, fish stock, tomato paste, sugar, marjoram, oregano, and bay leaf. Simmer briskly until the sauce is thick but still slightly liquid, 10 to 15 minutes.

As soon as the sauce starts simmering, season the fish and radicchio halves on both sides with salt and pepper and broil or grill, basting with the marinade, until the radicchio is golden brown, 3 to 5 minutes per side, and the fish is done to your liking, 5 to 7 minutes per side.

While the radicchio and tuna are cooking, bring a large pot of water to a boil. Cook the pasta until al dente, following manufacturer's suggested cooking time.

Remove and discard the bay leaf from the sauce. Stir in the arugula and cook until the leaves begin to wilt, about 1 minute more.

Drain the pasta and immediately toss with the sauce. Cut the tuna and radicchio into 1-inch chunks and scatter on top. Garnish with basil.

Serves 4

NUTRITIONAL ANALYSIS PER SERVING
Calories: 507   *Total fat:* 6.06 g
Saturated fat: .90 g   *Cholesterol:* 38 mg
Sodium: 289 mg

Tuna with Tomato and Fresh Dillweed

Chunks of water-packed tuna add satisfying flavor to a quickly prepared tomato sauce. The fresh dillweed shows off the seafood to good effect. If you like, add a few chopped leaves of fresh tarragon, too.

> ½ tablespoon olive oil
> 2 medium shallots, finely chopped
> 1 16-ounce can crushed tomatoes
> 1 tablespoon tomato paste
> 1 tablespoon sugar
> 1 tablespoon finely chopped fresh dillweed
> 1 tablespoon finely chopped fresh Italian parsley
> 1 bay leaf
> 1 long strip lemon zest, cut from a whole lemon with a
>   vegetable parer
> ¾ pound dried medium-sized shells or other shapes
> Salt and pepper
> 2 6-ounce cans white tuna in spring water, drained and
>   broken into ½- to 1-inch chunks

Bring a large pot of water to a boil.

Meanwhile, in a large nonstick saucepan or skillet, heat the olive oil with the shallots over moderate heat. When the shallots sizzle, add the tomatoes, tomato paste, sugar, dillweed, parsley, bay leaf, and lemon zest. Simmer the sauce briskly until it is thick but still slightly liquid, 10 to 15 minutes.

While the sauce is cooking, cook the pasta until al dente, following manufacturer's suggested cooking time.

When the sauce is almost ready, remove and discard the bay leaf and lemon zest. Season to taste with salt and pepper and stir in the tuna chunks, cooking 1 to 2 minutes more to heat them through.

As soon as the pasta is cooked, drain it and immediately toss with the sauce.

Serves 4

NUTRITIONAL ANALYSIS PER SERVING
Calories: 481   *Total fat:* 5.28 g
Saturated fat: .96 g   *Cholesterol:* 33 mg
Sodium: 535 mg

Grilled Cajun Swordfish with Chili Broth

If you like your seafood or pasta spicy, this dish aims to please you with its spicy rub for fresh swordfish fillets and the hint of fresh chili peppers gained by simmering them in rich fish stock.

½ teaspoon cayenne pepper
½ teaspoon mild paprika
½ teaspoon dried oregano, crumbled
½ teaspoon ground cumin
½ tablespoon olive oil
1 teaspoon lemon juice
1 pound skinless fresh swordfish fillets, cut into 4 pieces
3 cups rich salt-free fish stock
1 fresh small red serrano chili pepper, cut lengthwise into halves
1 fresh small green serrano chili pepper, cut lengthwise into halves
¾ pound dried fettuccine or tagliatelle
Salt and pepper
1 tablespoon finely chopped fresh Italian parsley
1 tablespoon finely chopped fresh chives

In a small bowl, stir together the cayenne, paprika, oregano, and cumin. Add the olive oil and lemon juice and stir to make a loose paste. Put the swordfish fillets in a shallow bowl and rub the paste evenly on both sides. Marinate at room temperature 15 to 30 minutes.

Meanwhile, bring a large pot of water to a boil. Preheat the broiler or grill until very hot.

Just before the water reaches a boil, put the fish stock and fresh chilies in a medium saucepan. Bring to a boil over high heat, then reduce the heat to medium and simmer until the stock reduces by about a third, 10 to 15 minutes.

As soon as the stock starts reducing, add the pasta to the boiling water and cook until al dente, following manufacturer's suggested cooking time.

At the same time, season the swordfish to taste with salt and pepper and broil or grill until cooked through but still moist, about 5 minutes per side.

Season the reduced fish stock to taste with salt and pepper and remove and discard the chilies. Drain the pasta and immediately place it in individual shallow serving bowls. Ladle the broth over the pasta and place the grilled swordfish on top. Garnish with parsley and chives.

Serves 4

NUTRITIONAL ANALYSIS PER SERVING
Calories: 488   *Total fat:* 7.69 g
Saturated fat: 1.65 g   *Cholesterol:* 44 mg
Sodium: 215 mg

Lemon-Dill Shrimp with Vodka Broth

In this presentation, vodka adds a splash of sophistication to quickly sautéed fresh shrimp. The alcohol evaporates during cooking.

¾ pound dried spaghetti or linguine
2 teaspoons unsalted butter
2 medium shallots, finely chopped
1 pound medium-sized fresh shrimp, peeled and deveined
Salt and white pepper
2 tablespoons vodka
1 tablespoon lemon juice
1 teaspoon finely grated lemon zest
½ cup rich salt-free fish stock
1 tablespoon finely chopped fresh chives

Bring a large pot of water to a boil. Add the pasta and cook until al dente, following manufacturer's suggested cooking time.

Meanwhile, in a large skillet, melt the butter with the shallots over moderate heat. As soon as the butter foams and the shallots sizzle, add the shrimp, seasoning to taste with salt and white pepper, and sauté until the shrimp turn uniformly pink, 1 to 2 minutes.

Add the vodka, lemon juice, and lemon zest. Raise the heat to high and continue cooking, stirring constantly, for about 1 minute more, until most of the liquid has evaporated.

Stir in the fish stock and bring the liquid back to a boil. Season to taste with salt and pepper.

Drain the pasta and immediately top with the shrimp and broth. Garnish with chives.

Serves 4

NUTRITIONAL ANALYSIS PER SERVING
Calories: 453   *Total fat:* 4.85 g
Saturated fat: 1.68 g   *Cholesterol:* 145 mg
Sodium: 161 mg

∽

Chili-Rubbed Shrimp with Santa Fe Tomato Sauce

This contemporary presentation draws on the flavors of old New Mexico, flavoring a tomato sauce with earthy dried red chilies and using it as the background for quickly broiled shrimp mildly seasoned with chili powder.

½ tablespoon olive oil

4 large dried red chili pods, split open, seeds and stems removed, pods cut with scissors into ½-inch pieces

1 small green bell pepper, halved, stemmed, seeded, and cut into ½-inch pieces

2 medium garlic cloves, finely chopped

1 16-ounce can crushed tomatoes

1 tablespoon tomato paste

1 tablespoon sugar

2 teaspoons dried oregano

1 bay leaf

1 pound medium-sized fresh shrimp, shelled and deveined

2 tablespoons lime juice

Olive oil-flavored nonstick cooking spray

1 tablespoon mild pure red chili powder

1 tablespoon sweet paprika

Salt and pepper

¾ pound dried spaghetti or linguine

1 tablespoon finely chopped fresh cilantro

Bring a large pot of water to a boil and preheat the broiler or grill until very hot.

Meanwhile, in a large nonstick skillet, heat the olive oil over moderate heat. Add the dried red chili, bell pepper, and garlic and, as soon as they give off their aromas, stir in the tomatoes, tomato paste, sugar, oregano, and bay leaf. Simmer the sauce until it is thick but still slightly liquid, about 15 minutes.

While the sauce is cooking, toss the shrimp with the lime juice and spray the shrimp lightly but evenly with the nonstick cooking spray. Then sprinkle evenly with the chili powder, paprika, and salt and pepper to taste.

Add the pasta to the boiling water and cook until al dente, following manufacturer's suggested cooking time.

While the pasta and sauce cook, broil the shrimp until done, 1 to 1½ minutes per side.

Remove and discard the bay leaf from the sauce and season the sauce to taste with salt and pepper. Drain the pasta and immediately toss with the sauce. Arrange the shrimp on top. Garnish with cilantro.

Serves 4

NUTRITIONAL ANALYSIS PER SERVING
Calories: 500   *Total fat:* 6.51 g
Saturated fat: .87 g   *Cholesterol:* 140 mg
Sodium: 382 mg

Sautéed Shrimp with Roasted Red Bell Peppers

Roasted peppers are so juicy that they practically form their own sauce. Red peppers provide a particularly beautiful background for shrimp quickly sautéed with garlic. But you could use other colors of pepper if you like, or even a mix of hues.

> ¾ pound dried fettuccine or tagliatelle
> ½ tablespoon olive oil
> 2 medium garlic cloves, finely chopped
> 1 pound medium shrimp, peeled and deveined
> ½ cup rich salt-free fish stock
> 4 medium-sized red bell peppers, roasted, peeled,
>   stemmed, and seeded (see page 7), and torn into
>   ¼-inch-wide strips, juices reserved
> Salt and pepper
> 2 tablespoons finely chopped fresh chives
> 2 tablespoons finely chopped fresh parsley

Bring a large pot of water to a boil. Add the pasta and cook until al dente, following manufacturer's suggested cooking time.

Meanwhile, in a large nonstick skillet, heat the olive oil with the garlic over moderate-to-high heat. When the garlic sizzles, add the shrimp and sauté until the shrimp turn uniformly pink, 1 to 2 minutes.

Add the fish stock and bell peppers and their juices and continue sautéing until much of the liquid has evaporated, 3 to 5 minutes more. Season to taste with salt and pepper.

Drain the pasta and immediately toss with the pepper-and-shrimp mixture. Garnish with chives and parsley.

Serves 4

NUTRITIONAL ANALYSIS PER SERVING
Calories: 454   *Total fat:* 4.75 g
Saturated fat: .72 g   *Cholesterol:* 140 mg
Sodium: 162 mg

❧

Seared Sea Scallops in
Shallot Broth with Chives

At once light on the palate and full-flavored, this dish has surprising elegance.

> 1 tablespoon olive oil
> 4 medium shallots, thinly sliced
> 4 cups rich salt-free fish stock
> ¾ pound dried angel hair or spaghettini
> 1 pound large fresh sea scallops, trimmed
> Salt and pepper
> 2 tablespoons fresh chives cut into ½-inch-long pieces

Bring a large pot of water to a boil.

In a large nonstick saucepan, heat ½ tablespoon of the olive oil over moderate heat. Add the shallots and sauté just until they begin to turn golden, 2 to 3 minutes. Add the fish stock, raise the heat, and bring to a boil. Continue boiling briskly until the stock has reduced to about 3 cups, 10 to 15 minutes.

About halfway through reducing the stock, add the pasta to the boiling water and cook until al dente, following the manufacturer's suggested cooking time.

When the pasta and stock are almost ready, in a large nonstick skillet, heat the remaining olive oil over moderate-to-high heat. Season the scallops on both sides to taste with salt and pepper and cook them until seared golden, 1 to 1½ minutes per side.

Season the reduced stock to taste with salt and pepper. Drain the pasta and immediately mound in individual shallow serving bowls. Ladle the stock and shallots over the pasta. Arrange the seared scallops on top. Garnish with chives.

Serves 4

NUTRITIONAL ANALYSIS PER SERVING
Calories: 472　　　　*Total fat:* 5.57 g
Saturated fat: .73 g　*Cholesterol:* 37 mg
Sodium: 330 mg

Grilled Scallops with
Roasted Red Pepper Pesto

What a pretty and tempting picture this dish presents: ivory-colored scallops against a vivid red pasta sauce that complements their natural sweetness and succulence.

> 2 tablespoons lemon juice
> ½ tablespoon olive oil
> 1 pound large fresh sea scallops, trimmed
> 4 medium red bell peppers, roasted, peeled, stemmed, and
>   seeded (see page 7), juices reserved
> 1 medium garlic clove, pared
> ½ cup concentrated fat-free chicken broth (see page 4)
> 2 tablespoons grated Romano cheese
> 1 tablespoon finely shredded fresh basil leaves
> ½ tablespoon chopped fresh Italian parsley
> ½ teaspoon sugar
> Salt and white pepper
> ¾ pound dried angel hair or spaghettini
> 8 whole chives, cut into 1-inch pieces

In a small bowl, combine 1 tablespoon of the lemon juice with the olive oil. Add the scallops and turn them in the mixture to coat evenly. Marinate at room temperature for 15 to 30 minutes.

Meanwhile, preheat the broiler or grill until very hot. Bring a large pot of water to a boil.

At the same time, put the peppers and their juices, the garlic, 6 tablespoons of the concentrated chicken broth, the remaining lemon juice, the Romano cheese, basil, parsley, and sugar in a food processor fitted with the metal blade. Pulse the ingredients until they are coarsely chopped, then scrape down the work bowl and process until the mixture is smoothly pureed, adding more of the broth if necessary to achieve a thick but slightly fluid consistency. Season to taste with salt and white pepper. Set aside.

Add the pasta to the boiling water and cook until al dente, following manufacturer's suggested cooking time.

While the pasta is cooking, season the scallops to taste with salt and pepper and broil or grill them close to the heat until golden, 1 to 2 minutes per side.

Drain the pasta and immediately toss with the pesto. Place the scallops on top. Garnish with chive pieces.

Serves 4

NUTRITIONAL ANALYSIS PER SERVING
Calories: 475   *Total fat:* 4.72 g
Saturated fat: .51 g   *Cholesterol:* 40 mg
Sodium: 241 mg

Steamed Clams in Roasted Garlic Broth

Roasting garlic develops its rich, sweet flavor, adding extra subtlety to this simple presentation for fresh clams.

> 4 medium garlic cloves, left whole and unpared
> ½ tablespoon olive oil
> 2 cups rich salt-free fish stock
> ¾ pound dried linguine or spaghetti
> 3 dozen small fresh clams such as littlenecks or Manilas,
>   in the shell, thoroughly scrubbed and rinsed
> Salt and pepper
> 2 tablespoons finely chopped fresh chives
> 2 tablespoons thinly shredded fresh basil leaves

Preheat the oven to 375°F. Toss the garlic with the olive oil and seal securely in heavy-duty aluminum foil. Roast in the oven until tender, 30 to 40 minutes. Carefully unwrap the package and when the garlic is cool enough to handle, squeeze the soft cloves out of their skins and discard the skins.

Bring a large pot of water to a boil. In a large saucepan, put the garlic cloves with the fish stock and bring to a boil.

Add the pasta to the boiling water and cook until al dente, following manufacturer's suggested cooking time.

As soon as the fish stock comes to a boil, add the clams and cover the pan. Steam the clams until all have opened, 3 to 5 minutes; discard any unopened clams.

Drain the pasta. With a slotted spoon, remove the opened clams from the pan and place them on top of the pasta.

Line a wire strainer with a double thickness of cheesecloth and set it on top of a mixing bowl. Pour the fish stock through the strainer. Season to taste with salt and pepper. Ladle the stock over the clams and pasta. Garnish with chives and basil.

Serves 4

NUTRITIONAL ANALYSIS PER SERVING

Calories: 447   *Total fat:* 4.35 g
Saturated fat: .53 g   *Cholesterol:* 46 mg
Sodium: 152 mg

✌

Clams Arrabiata

A tomato sauce made "rabid" with red chili flakes and garlic shows off the taste of clams in this quickly prepared sauce. There's so much pleasurably intense flavor here that you'd never guess it's so low in fat.

½ tablespoon olive oil
4 medium garlic cloves, finely chopped
2 medium scallions, finely chopped
1 tablespoon crushed red pepper flakes
1 16-ounce can crushed tomatoes
½ cup dry red wine
1 tablespoon tomato paste
1 tablespoon sugar
½ tablespoon dried oregano
1 bay leaf
2 6½-ounce cans chopped clams, liquid saved
¾ pound dried linguine or spaghetti
Salt and pepper
2 tablespoons finely chopped fresh Italian parsley
1 tablespoon finely chopped fresh basil leaves

Bring a large pot of water to a boil.

Meanwhile, in a large nonstick skillet or saucepan, heat the olive oil with the garlic, scallions, and red pepper flakes over moderate heat. As soon as they give off their aromas, add the tomatoes, red wine, tomato paste, sugar, oregano, and bay leaf; strain and stir in the liquid from the canned clams, setting the clams aside.

Simmer the sauce briskly until it is thick but still slightly liquid, about 15 minutes.

While the sauce is cooking, add the pasta to the boiling water and cook until al dente, following manufacturer's suggested cooking time.

When the sauce is almost ready, remove and discard the bay leaf, stir in the clams and season to taste with salt and pepper. Continue cooking until the clams are heated through, 1 to 2 minutes more.

As soon as the pasta is cooked, drain it and immediately toss with the sauce. Garnish with parsley and basil.

Serves 4

NUTRITIONAL ANALYSIS PER SERVING
Calories: 477   *Total fat:* 4.57 g
Saturated fat: .59 g   *Cholesterol:* 32 mg
Sodium: 281 mg

❧

Creamy White-Wine Clam Sauce

The "creaminess" in this light version of a favorite Italian seafood sauce comes from evaporated skimmed milk.

¾ pound dried linguine or spaghetti
2 6½-ounce cans chopped clams, liquid saved
½ tablespoon cornstarch
1 tablespoon olive oil
2 medium garlic cloves, finely chopped
2 medium shallots, finely chopped
½ cup evaporated skimmed milk
½ cup dry white wine
1 bay leaf
Salt and pepper
2 tablespoons finely chopped fresh Italian parsley
2 tablespoons finely chopped fresh basil leaves

Bring a large pot of water to a boil. Add the pasta and cook until al dente, following manufacturer's suggested cooking time.

In a cup or small bowl, put the liquid from the canned clams; sprinkle and stir in the cornstarch and set aside.

Meanwhile, in a large nonstick saucepan or skillet, heat the olive oil with the garlic and shallots over moderate heat. When they sizzle, add the evaporated milk, white wine, and bay leaf. Bring to a boil and reduce the heat to a bare simmer.

Briefly restir the cornstarch-clam liquid mixture and pour it into the pan, continuing to stir until the sauce thickens to a light, creamy consistency. Stir in the clams and cook about 1 minute more. Remove and discard the bay leaf, season to taste with salt and pepper, and stir in the parsley and basil.

Drain the pasta and immediately toss with the sauce.

Serves 4

NUTRITIONAL ANALYSIS PER SERVING
Calories: 474   *Total fat:* 5.74 g
Saturated fat: .76 g   *Cholesterol:* 33 mg
Sodium: 100 mg

Mussels with Lemon Zest–Tomato Broth

The natural sweetness of mussels is highlighted by the generous measure of lemon zest, and the tomatoes contrast beautifully with the mussels' gleaming black shells to produce a dish as beautiful to look at as it is delicious to eat.

½ tablespoon olive oil
2 medium garlic cloves, finely chopped
2 medium shallots, finely chopped
2 cups rich salt-free fish stock
1 bay leaf
32 small fresh mussels in the shell, rinsed clean and debearded
¾ pound dried spaghetti or linguine
6 medium Roma tomatoes, cored, halved, seeded (see page 8),
    and coarsely chopped
2 teaspoons finely grated lemon zest
Salt and pepper
2 tablespoons finely shredded fresh basil leaves
2 tablespoons finely chopped fresh Italian parsley

Bring a large pot of water to a boil.

In another large pot or nonstick saucepan, heat the olive oil with the garlic and shallots over moderate heat. When they sizzle, add the fish stock and bay leaf and bring to a boil. Add the mussels, cover, and steam until the mussels have opened, 2 to 3 minutes. Discard any unopened mussels. With a slotted spoon, remove the mussels and keep them warm in a covered bowl.

Add the pasta to the boiling water and cook until al dente, following manufacturer's suggested cooking time.

Meanwhile, line a wire strainer with a double thickness of cheesecloth and set it over a mixing bowl. Pour the contents of the mussel cooking pot through the strainer. Rinse out the pot and return the strained liquid to the pot.

Bring the liquid back to a simmer over medium heat. Add the tomatoes and lemon zest and continue cooking until the tomatoes are heated through and the liquid has colored the broth, 2 to 3 minutes. Season to taste with salt and pepper, add the basil and parsley, and return the mussels to the pan to warm them through, about 1 minute more.

Drain the pasta and spoon the sauce, complete with the mussels in their shells, over it.

Serves 4

NUTRITIONAL ANALYSIS PER SERVING
Calories: 404   *Total fat:* 4.32 g
Saturated fat: .64 g   *Cholesterol:* 13 mg
Sodium: 220 mg

♋

Seafood Celebration

For those who love seafood in all its variety, this quick, light sauce perfectly satisfies their cravings. Vary the seafood you include as your own tastes dictate.

1 tablespoon olive oil
1 medium green bell pepper, stemmed, seeded, and
   cut into ¼-inch dice
2 medium shallots, finely chopped
1 medium garlic clove, finely chopped
1 teaspoon whole fennel seeds
¼ teaspoon crushed red pepper flakes
1 cup rich salt-free fish stock
1 16-ounce can crushed tomatoes
1 tablespoon tomato paste
1 teaspoon sugar
1 teaspoon dried oregano
1 teaspoon dried thyme
1 bay leaf
¾ pound dried linguine, spaghetti, or medium-sized pasta shapes
¼ pound swordfish fillet, cut into ½-inch chunks
¼ pound bay scallops
¼ pound small fresh shrimp, peeled and deveined
2 baby squids, cleaned, bodies cut crosswise into thin rings,
   tentacles cut into small clusters
Salt and pepper

Bring a large pot of water to a boil.

Meanwhile, in a large nonstick skillet or saucepan, heat the olive oil with the green pepper, shallots, garlic, fennel, and red pepper flakes over moderate heat. When they give off their aromas, add the fish stock, raise the heat to high, and boil until reduced by about a third, about 5 minutes.

Stir in the tomatoes, tomato paste, sugar, oregano, thyme, and bay leaf. Reduce the heat slightly and simmer briskly until the sauce is thick but still slightly liquid, about 10 to 12 minutes more.

About halfway through the sauce's simmering time, add the pasta to the boiling water and cook until al dente, following manufacturer's suggested cooking time.

Add the seafood to the reduced sauce and simmer, stirring gently, until the seafood is just cooked through, about 5 minutes. Remove and discard the bay leaf. Season to taste with salt and pepper.

Drain the pasta and immediately toss with the sauce.

Serves 4

NUTRITIONAL ANALYSIS PER SERVING
Calories: 531   *Total fat:* 7.70 g
Saturated fat: 1.28 g   *Cholesterol:* 187 mg
Sodium: 390 mg

6

Poultry and Meat

Grilled Chicken with Mixed Herb–Lemon Pesto

Chicken Breast with Peas in Sherry Cream Sauce

Grilled Chicken with Curried Tomato Sauce

Chicken in Leek Cream Sauce with Sun-Dried Tomatoes

Ground Turkey Curry

Spicy Turkey Sausage and Roasted Peppers

Turkey and Bell Pepper Bolognese Picante

Chunky Lean Beef with Spring Vegetables

Light Diner-Style Chili and Cheese

Lean Beef Lasagna

Lean Classic Bolognese with Beef and Pork

Grilled Lamb Tenderloin with Rosemary-Pepper Pesto

Bolognese-Style Ground Lamb and Fresh Rosemary

Diced Canadian Bacon with Lentils

Canadian Bolognese

Stir-Fried Pork Tenderloin with Shiitake Mushrooms and Scallions

New Mexican Green Chili Pork and Tomatoes

Lean Pork Meatballs with Fresh Tomato Sauce

Grilled Pork Tenderloin with Barbecue-Tomato Sauce

Pork Fajita Stir-Fry

❧

Grilled Chicken with
Mixed Herb–Lemon Pesto

If you like traditional Genovese-style pesto, you'll find this sauce a refreshing change of pace and a vibrant companion to grilled chicken breast strips. Try the sauce on its own, if you like, substituting concentrated vegetable broth for a completely vegetarian version.

¼ cup lemon juice
1 tablespoon olive oil
1 pound boneless skinless chicken breasts
¾ pound dried fettuccine or tagliatelle
2 cups packed stemmed fresh basil leaves
¼ cup packed fresh Italian parsley leaves
3 tablespoons toasted pine nuts (see page 7)
3 tablespoons finely grated lemon zest
2 tablespoons finely chopped fresh chives
2 tablespoons finely chopped fresh dillweed
2 tablespoons grated Romano cheese
1 medium garlic clove, finely chopped
½ cup concentrated fat-free chicken broth (see page 4)
Salt and pepper

In a shallow bowl, stir together the lemon juice and olive oil. Add the chicken breasts and turn them in the mixture to coat evenly. Marinate at room temperature for 30 minutes.

Meanwhile, preheat the broiler or grill until very hot. Bring a large pot of water to a boil.

Broil or grill the chicken until golden, about 7 minutes per side.

After the chicken starts cooking, add the pasta to the boiling water and cook until al dente, following manufacturer's suggested cooking time.

While the chicken and pasta cook, put the basil, parsley, pine nuts, lemon zest, chives, dillweed, Romano cheese, garlic, and half of the concentrated chicken broth in a food processor fitted with the metal blade. Pulse the ingredients until they are coarsely chopped, then scrape down the work bowl and process until the mixture is smoothly pureed, adding more of the broth if necessary to achieve a thick but slightly fluid consistency. Season the sauce to taste with salt and pepper.

Drain the pasta and immediately toss with the pesto. Cut the chicken crosswise into ¼-inch-wide strips and place the strips on top.

Serves 4

NUTRITIONAL ANALYSIS PER SERVING
Calories: 568   *Total fat:* 10.80 g
Saturated fat: 1.53 g *Cholesterol:* 68 mg
Sodium: 140 mg

Chicken Breast with Peas in Sherry Cream Sauce

Soothingly old-fashioned, this dish is also good made with turkey breast. If you'd like a little more spice, substitute hot paprika for the mild. Other vegetables, such as button mushrooms, bell peppers, or diced carrot, also may be added at the same time or in place of the peas. For a change of pace, try this over the rice-shaped pasta known as orzo.

¾ pound dried fettuccine or tagliatelle
½ tablespoon vegetable oil
1 small onion, finely chopped
1 small garlic clove, finely chopped
1 pound boneless skinless chicken breast halves,
     cut crosswise into ¼-inch-thick slices
½ teaspoon mild paprika
¼ cup dry sherry
1 cup concentrated fat-free chicken broth (see page 4)
¾ pound fresh peas, shelled (about 1 cup peas)
½ cup nonfat milk
1 tablespoon cornstarch
Salt and pepper
2 tablespoons finely chopped fresh chives

Bring a large pot of water to a boil. Add the pasta and cook until al dente, following manufacturer's suggested cooking time.

Meanwhile, in a nonstick skillet, heat the vegetable oil with the onion and garlic over moderate-to-high heat. As soon as they sizzle, add the chicken, sprinkle with the paprika, and sauté until the pieces lose their pink color, 2 to 3 minutes.

Raise the heat to high, add the sherry, and sauté about 1 minute more. Add the concentrated chicken broth and the peas and cook until the peas are tender and the chicken is cooked through, about 5 minutes more.

While the peas and chicken are cooking, put the milk in a small cup or bowl and sprinkle and stir in the cornstarch until dissolved. Pour the cornstarch mixture into the pan and continue stirring until the sauce thickens, developing a creamy consistency, 1 to 2 minutes more.

Drain the pasta. Season the sauce to taste with salt and pepper and toss the pasta with the sauce. Garnish with chives.

Serves 4

NUTRITIONAL ANALYSIS PER SERVING
Calories: 559   *Total fat:* 4.71 g
Saturated fat: .82 g   *Cholesterol:* 66 mg
Sodium: 138 mg

ᔥ

Grilled Chicken with Curried Tomato Sauce

A hint of mild curry adds intrigue to the sauce that backs up these quickly seared strips of chicken breast. Seek out a good-quality imported Indian curry powder.

¼ cup orange juice
2 tablespoons lemon juice
1 tablespoon vegetable oil
1 pound boneless skinless chicken breasts
1 small onion, finely chopped
2 medium garlic cloves, finely chopped
1 tablespoon finely grated fresh gingerroot
1½ tablespoons mild curry powder
1 16-ounce can crushed tomatoes
1 tablespoon tomato paste
1 tablespoon sugar
1 teaspoon whole fennel seeds
¾ pound dried linguine or fettuccine
Salt and pepper
¼ cup finely chopped fresh cilantro or parsley

In a large, shallow dish, stir together the orange and lemon juices and ½ tablespoon of the vegetable oil. Add the chicken breasts and turn them in the mixture to coat evenly. Marinade at room temperature for 30 minutes.

Meanwhile, preheat the broiler or grill until very hot. Bring a large pot of water to a boil.

At the same time, in a large nonstick skillet or saucepan, heat the remaining vegetable oil with the onion, garlic, and gingerroot over moderate heat. As soon as they sizzle, sprinkle in the curry powder and sauté until they give off their aromas, about 1 minute. Add the tomatoes, tomato paste, sugar, and fennel. Simmer until the sauce is thick but still slightly liquid, 10 to 15 minutes.

While the sauce is simmering, add the pasta to the boiling water and cook until al dente, following manufacturer's suggested cooking time.

Season the chicken breasts with salt and pepper to taste. Broil or grill until cooked through and golden brown, 4 to 5 minutes per side.

Drain the pasta. Season the sauce to taste with salt and pepper, stir in the cilantro or parsley, and toss with the pasta.

Cut the chicken breasts crosswise into ¼- to ½-inch-thick slices and arrange them on top of the pasta.

Serves 4

NUTRITIONAL ANALYSIS PER SERVING
Calories: 541   *Total fat:* 6.90 g
Saturated fat: 1.03 g *Cholesterol:* 66 mg
Sodium: 302 mg

Chicken in Leek Cream Sauce with Sun-Dried Tomatoes

You'll find this sauce especially lovely to look at, with its strips of pale-green leek, ivory-colored chicken, and brick-red tomatoes offset by a creamy sauce. The flavor combination is equally pleasing.

1 tablespoon butter
2 medium leeks, trimmed, cut lengthwise into halves,
  thoroughly washed, and cut crosswise into ⅛-inch-thick slices
2 medium garlic cloves, finely chopped
1 pound boneless skinless chicken breasts, cut crosswise
  into ¼-inch-thick strips
Salt and pepper
¾ pound dried linguine, fettuccine, or tagliatelle
½ cup dry white wine
12 dry-packed sun-dried tomatoes, cut into ¼-inch-wide strips
1 cup evaporated skimmed milk
2 tablespoons finely chopped fresh Italian parsley

Bring a large pot of water to a boil.

Meanwhile, in a large nonstick skillet, melt the butter over moderate heat. Add the leeks and garlic and sauté about 1 minute. Add the chicken, seasoning to taste with salt and pepper, and continue sautéing until the strips lose their pink color, about 5 minutes more.

Add the pasta to the boiling water and cook until al dente, following manufacturer's suggested cooking time.

Meanwhile, add the wine and sun-dried tomatoes to the skillet, raise the heat to high and simmer briskly until the wine reduces to a few tablespoons, about 5 minutes. Stir in the evaporated milk and continue simmering, stirring occasionally, until it reduces to a thick, creamy consistency, 5 to 7 minutes more. Season to taste with salt and pepper.

Drain the pasta and immediately toss with the sauce. Garnish with parsley.

Serves 4

NUTRITIONAL ANALYSIS PER SERVING
Calories: 579   *Total fat:* 6.17 g
Saturated fat: 2.46 g   *Cholesterol:* 76 mg
Sodium: 207 mg

Ground Turkey Curry

This mild tomato-based curry, with its complementary hint of sweetness, is intensely satisfying. If your butcher doesn't sell ground turkey, buy boneless skinless turkey breast and ask to have it ground for you, or cut it into chunks and chop it at home in your food processor (see page 6).

1 tablespoon olive oil
1 small onion, finely chopped
1 medium garlic clove, finely chopped
2 tablespoons curry powder
¾ pound ground turkey breast
¼ cup medium-dry white wine
1 16-ounce can crushed tomatoes
2 tablespoons seedless golden or brown raisins
1 tablespoon tomato paste
2 teaspoons sugar
1 cinnamon stick
1 bay leaf
¾ pound dried spaghetti, fettuccine, or
    medium-sized shells or tubes
Salt and pepper
1 tablespoon finely chopped fresh cilantro leaves

In a large nonstick saucepan or skillet, heat the olive oil with the onion and garlic over moderate heat. When they sizzle, stir in the curry powder. Add the turkey and sauté it, stirring and breaking up the meat with a wooden spoon, until it begins to brown, 5 to 7 minutes.

Add the wine and stir and scrape well to deglaze the pan. Add the tomatoes and stir in the raisins, tomato paste, sugar, cinnamon stick, and bay leaf. Simmer the sauce until thick but still slightly liquid, 20 to 25 minutes.

Meanwhile, bring a large pot of water to a boil. Add the pasta and cook until al dente, following manufacturer's suggested cooking time.

When the sauce is ready, remove and discard the bay leaf and cinnamon stick. Season to taste with salt and pepper. Drain the pasta and immediately toss with the sauce. Garnish with cilantro.

Serves 4

NUTRITIONAL ANALYSIS PER SERVING

Calories: 512   *Total fat:* 6.07 g
Saturated fat: .85 g   *Cholesterol:* 53 mg
Sodium: 269 mg

Spicy Turkey Sausage and Roasted Peppers

A classic Italian combination, sausage and peppers finds new lightness with the use of lean turkey sausage. Seek out one of the many varieties of fresh sausage being made today and sold in well-stocked markets and specialty butcher shops. Opt for a spicy Italian-style sausage, or go with a sweeter, milder version if you like—or, for that matter, a similar chicken sausage.

¾ pound dried fettuccine or tagliatelle
½ tablespoon olive oil
2 medium garlic cloves, finely chopped
¾ pound fresh spicy Italian-style turkey sausage,
    casings split, peeled off and discarded, meat coarsely crumbled
1 medium green bell pepper, roasted, stemmed, peeled, and seeded
    (see page 7), juices reserved, flesh torn into ¼-inch-wide strips
1 medium red bell pepper, roasted, stemmed, peeled, and seeded
    (see page 7), juices reserved, flesh torn into ¼-inch-wide strips
1 medium yellow bell pepper, roasted, stemmed, peeled, and seeded
    (see page 7), juices reserved, flesh torn into ¼-inch-wide strips
2 tablespoons balsamic vinegar
1 tablespoon finely shredded fresh basil leaves
1 tablespoon finely chopped fresh Italian parsley
1 teaspoon dried oregano
Salt and pepper

Bring a large pot of water to a boil. Add the pasta and cook until al dente, following manufacturer's suggested cooking time.

Meanwhile, in a large nonstick skillet, heat the olive oil and garlic over moderate-to-high heat. When the garlic sizzles, add the sausage and cook until uniformly browned, 5 to 7 minutes.

Add the peppers and their juices, the balsamic vinegar, basil, parsley, and oregano and continue to sauté, stirring, until the ingredients are well combined and thoroughly heated through, about 2 minutes more. Season to taste with salt and pepper.

Drain the pasta and immediately toss with the sauce.

Serves 4

NUTRITIONAL ANALYSIS PER SERVING
Calories: 492   *Total fat:* 12.15 g
Saturated fat: 3.41 g   *Cholesterol:* 65 mg
Sodium: 531 mg

Turkey and Bell Pepper Bolognese Picante

*A splash of rich-tasting balsamic vinegar adds a tangy dimension to comple-
ment the sweet bell peppers and the hint of hot crushed red chili in this sauce.*

½ tablespoon olive oil
1 medium onion, finely chopped
2 medium garlic cloves, finely chopped
*1 medium red bell pepper, halved, stemmed, seeded,
    and cut into ½-inch dice*
*1 medium green bell pepper, halved, stemmed, seeded,
    and cut into ½-inch dice*
½ teaspoon crushed red pepper flakes
¾ pound ground turkey breast
2 tablespoons balsamic vinegar
1 16-ounce can salt-free crushed tomatoes
1 tablespoon tomato paste
½ tablespoon sugar
1 teaspoon dried oregano
½ teaspoon dried thyme
½ teaspoon dried marjoram
1 bay leaf
*¾ pound dried rigatoni, mostaccioli, or other medium-sized
    to large pasta shapes*
1 tablespoon finely chopped fresh Italian parsley
Salt and pepper

In a large nonstick saucepan or skillet, heat the olive oil with the onion, garlic, bell peppers, and pepper flakes over moderate heat. When they sizzle, add the turkey and sauté it, stirring and breaking up the meat into fine particles with a wooden spoon, until it just begins to brown, 5 to 7 minutes.

Add the balsamic vinegar and stir and scrape well to deglaze the pan deposits. Add the tomatoes; stir in the tomato paste, sugar, oregano, thyme, marjoram, and bay leaf.

Simmer the sauce, stirring occasionally, until thick but still slightly liquid, 20 to 25 minutes.

While the sauce is cooking, bring a large pot of water to a boil. Add the pasta and cook until al dente, following manufacturer's suggested cooking time.

When the sauce is ready, remove and discard the bay leaf and add the parsley. Season to taste with salt and pepper. Drain the pasta and immediately toss with the sauce.

Serves 4

NUTRITIONAL ANALYSIS PER SERVING
Calories: 490   *Total fat:* 4.08 g
Saturated fat: .63 g   *Cholesterol:* 53 mg
Sodium: 98 mg

Chunky Lean Beef with Spring Vegetables

Abundant shreds of vegetables fleck the tomato-based sauce in this colorful dish, complementing hearty-tasting chunks of lean ground beef.

> ½ tablespoon olive oil
> 2 medium shallots, finely chopped
> ¾ pound extralean ground beef
> 1 16-ounce can crushed tomatoes
> ½ cup concentrated fat-free beef broth (see page 4)
> 1 tablespoon tomato paste
> 2 teaspoons sugar
> 1 teaspoon dried oregano
> 1 teaspoon dried marjoram
> 1 teaspoon dried thyme
> 1 bay leaf
> ¾ pound dried farfalle or other medium-sized pasta shapes
> 1 medium carrot, coarsely shredded
> 1 medium zucchini, coarsely shredded
> 1 cup packed fresh baby spinach leaves, thoroughly washed
>   and coarsely shredded
> Salt and pepper
> 1 tablespoon finely shredded fresh basil leaves
> 1 tablespoon finely chopped fresh Italian parsley

Bring a large pot of water to a boil.

Meanwhile, in a large nonstick saucepan or skillet, heat the olive oil with the shallots over moderate heat. When the shallots sizzle, add the beef and sauté it, using a wooden spoon to break up the meat into coarse chunks, until it begins to brown, 5 to 7 minutes.

Pour off any excess fat from the pan. Stir in the tomatoes, concentrated beef broth, tomato paste, sugar, oregano, marjoram, thyme, and bay leaf. Simmer until the sauce is thick but still slightly liquid, 15 to 20 minutes.

About halfway through the sauce's cooking time, add the pasta to the boiling water and cook until al dente, following manufacturer's suggested cooking time.

A few minutes before the pasta is cooked, stir the carrot, zucchini, and spinach shreds into the sauce and continue cooking until they are al dente. Remove and discard the bay leaf and season the sauce to taste with salt and pepper.

Drain the pasta and immediately toss it with the sauce. Garnish with basil and parsley.

Serves 4

NUTRITIONAL ANALYSIS PER SERVING
Calories: 541   *Total fat:* 12.06 g
Saturated fat: 3.86 g *Cholesterol:* 53 mg
Sodium: 327 mg

Light Diner-Style Chili and Cheese

People attempting to follow healthier diets sometimes find themselves yearning for old-fashioned diner favorites that they're no longer allowed. This recipe re-creates an old lunch-counter favorite, while trimming away excess fat.

½ tablespoon olive oil
2 medium onions, finely chopped
2 medium garlic cloves, finely chopped
½ pound extralean ground beef
2 teaspoons chili powder
2 teaspoons cayenne pepper
1 teaspoon ground cumin
1 16-ounce can crushed tomatoes
1 8¾-ounce can kidney beans, drained
1 tablespoon tomato paste
½ tablespoon dark brown sugar
½ tablespoon dried oregano
1 bay leaf
¾ pound dried spaghetti
Salt and pepper
⅛ teaspoon hot chili sauce
¼ pound fat-free sharp cheddar cheese, grated
1 small red onion, finely chopped

Bring a large pot of water to a boil.

Meanwhile, in a large nonstick skillet or saucepan, heat the olive oil over moderate heat. Add the onions and garlic and sauté until translucent, 2 to 3 minutes. Add the beef and sauté, stirring and breaking up the meat into fine particles with a wooden spoon, until evenly browned, 5 to 7 minutes. Stir in the chili powder, cayenne, and cumin and sauté about 1 minute more.

Add the tomatoes, kidney beans, tomato paste, brown sugar, oregano, and bay leaf. Simmer briskly until thick but still slightly liquid, 10 to 15 minutes.

Meanwhile, add the pasta to the boiling water and cook until al dente, following manufacturer's suggested cooking time.

Remove and discard the bay leaf from the sauce and season the sauce to taste with salt and pepper. Stir in the hot chili sauce.

Drain the pasta and ladle the sauce on top. Garnish with grated cheddar cheese and chopped red onion.

Serves 4

NUTRITIONAL ANALYSIS PER SERVING
Calories: 601   *Total fat:* 10.02 g
Saturated fat: 2.78 g   *Cholesterol:* 40 mg
Sodium: 564 mg

Lean Beef Lasagna

Robust as this lasagna is, you'd be hard-pressed to believe that it's a light version of the trattoria favorite.

⅓ pound dried lasagna noodles
1 tablespoon olive oil
2 medium garlic cloves, finely chopped
¾ pound extralean ground beef
1 16-ounce can crushed tomatoes
1 tablespoon tomato paste
2 teaspoons sugar
1 teaspoon dried basil
1 teaspoon dried oregano
Salt and pepper
15 ounces fat-free ricotta cheese
¼ cup grated Romano cheese
2 egg whites, lightly beaten
Nonstick cooking spray
½ pound fat-free mozzarella or Monterey Jack cheese,
    coarsely shredded

Bring a large pot of water to a boil. Add the pasta and cook until al dente, following manufacturer's suggested cooking time. Drain.

Meanwhile, in a large nonstick skillet or saucepan, heat the olive oil with the garlic over moderate heat. When the garlic sizzles, add the beef and sauté, stirring and breaking up the meat into fine particles with a wooden spoon, until it uniformly loses its red color, about 5 minutes. Add the tomatoes, tomato paste, sugar, basil, and oregano and simmer until the sauce is thick but still slightly liquid, 10 to 15 minutes. Season to taste with salt and pepper and set aside.

In a mixing bowl, stir together the ricotta and Romano cheeses and the egg whites. Season to taste with salt and pepper.

Preheat the oven to 375°F.

Lightly spray a deep 8-inch-square baking dish with nonstick cooking spray. Lightly spoon a little of the liquid from the meat sauce on the bottom of the dish. Arrange one third of the cooked pasta on top, trimming the noodles to fit. Spread one-third of the meat sauce on the noodles, then a third of the ricotta mixture, and a third of the mozzarella. Repeat in that order until all the ingredients are used, ending with the mozzarella.

Cover the dish loosely with foil, not touching the mozzarella, and bake for about 30 minutes. Remove the foil and bake 20 to 30 minutes more, until the lasagna is bubbly and the top is golden. Remove from the oven and let the lasagna settle for 5 to 10 minutes before slicing and serving.

Serves 4

NUTRITIONAL ANALYSIS PER SERVING
Calories: 556   *Total fat:* 14.40 g
Saturated fat: 3.96 g   *Cholesterol:* 68 mg
Sodium: 981 mg

❧

Lean Classic Bolognese with Beef and Pork

Rich and meaty, this traditional sauce stays light by calling for only the leanest cuts. You'll ensure the healthiest results by buying the meat whole and trimming and chopping it yourself at home.

½ tablespoon olive oil
1 medium onion, finely chopped
2 medium garlic cloves, finely chopped
6 ounces beef tenderloin, trimmed of all visible fat
    and chopped in a food processor (see page 6)
6 ounces pork tenderloin, trimmed of all visible fat
    and chopped in a food processor (see page 6)
¼ cup dry red wine
¼ cup concentrated fat-free beef broth (see page 4)
1 tablespoon balsamic vinegar
1 16-ounce can crushed tomatoes
1 tablespoon tomato paste
2 teaspoons sugar
1 tablespoon dried oregano
1 bay leaf
¾ pound dried spaghetti, penne, or medium-sized shells
1 tablespoon finely chopped fresh Italian parsley
1 tablespoon finely shredded fresh basil leaves
Salt and pepper

In a large nonstick saucepan or skillet, heat the olive oil with the onion and garlic over moderate heat. When they sizzle, add the beef and pork. Sauté, stirring and breaking up the meat with a wooden spoon, until the meat begins to brown, 5 to 7 minutes.

Add the wine, concentrated beef broth, and balsamic vinegar and stir and scrape well to deglaze the pan deposits. Stir in the tomatoes, tomato paste, sugar, oregano, and bay leaf. Simmer until the sauce is thick but still slightly liquid, 20 to 25 minutes.

Meanwhile, bring a large pot of water to a boil. Add the pasta and cook until al dente, following manufacturer's suggested cooking time.

When the sauce is ready, remove and discard the bay leaf and stir in the parsley and basil. Season to taste with salt and pepper. Drain the pasta and immediately toss with the sauce.

Serves 4

NUTRITIONAL ANALYSIS PER SERVING
Calories: 512   *Total fat:* 8.32 g
Saturated fat: 2.23 g   *Cholesterol:* 54 mg
Sodium: 279 mg

❧

Grilled Lamb Tenderloin with Rosemary-Pepper Pesto

Surprisingly lean lamb tenderloin gets the elegant accompaniment of a thick bell-pepper sauce and a bed of pasta. Try this with pork tenderloin, too.

2 tablespoons lemon juice
½ tablespoon olive oil
1 pound lamb tenderloin, trimmed of all visible fat
Salt and pepper
¾ pound dried angel hair or spaghettini
4 medium red bell peppers, roasted, stemmed, peeled, and seeded (see page 7), juices saved
1 medium garlic clove, pared
½ cup concentrated fat-free chicken broth (see page 4)
2 tablespoons grated Romano cheese
2 teaspoons fresh rosemary leaves, coarsely chopped
½ tablespoon chopped fresh Italian parsley
1 teaspoon sugar
4 small fresh rosemary sprigs

In a shallow bowl, stir together 1 tablespoon of the lemon juice with the olive oil. Add the lamb and turn it in the mixture to coat evenly. Marinate at room temperature, turning occasionally, for 30 minutes.

Meanwhile, preheat the broiler or grill until very hot. Bring a large pot of water to a boil.

Remove the lamb from the marinade and season to taste with salt and pepper. Broil or grill until well charred but still fairly rare inside, about 5 minutes per side.

While the lamb broils, add the pasta to the boiling water and cook until al dente, following manufacturer's suggested cooking time.

At the same time, put the peppers and their juices, the garlic, 6 table-spoons of the concentrated chicken broth, the remaining lemon juice, the Romano cheese, fresh rosemary leaves, parsley, and sugar in a food processor fitted with the metal blade. Pulse the ingredients until they are coarsely chopped, then scrape down the work bowl and process until the mixture is smoothly pureed, adding more of the broth if necessary to achieve a thick but slightly fluid consistency. Season to taste with salt and pepper.

When the lamb is cooked, cut it crosswise diagonally into ¼-inch-thick slices, saving the juices. Drain the pasta and immediately toss with the pesto. Drape the lamb slices on top and spoon the meat juices over the lamb. Garnish with rosemary sprigs.

Serves 4

NUTRITIONAL ANALYSIS PER SERVING
Calories: 560   *Total fat:* 12.15 g
Saturated fat: 3.38 g   *Cholesterol:* 83 mg
Sodium: 130 mg

꧁

Bolognese-Style Ground Lamb and Fresh Rosemary

Lamb and rosemary are natural partners, and the herb gives a lovely flavor to this interesting variation on a classic Italian meat sauce.

½ teaspoon olive oil
1 small onion, finely chopped
3 medium garlic cloves, finely chopped
¾ pound lamb loin, trimmed of all visible fat
    and chopped in a food processor (see page 6)
½ cup dry red wine
1 16-ounce can crushed tomatoes
1 tablespoon tomato paste
2 teaspoons finely chopped fresh rosemary leaves
½ tablespoon sugar
1 bay leaf
¾ pound dried tagliatelle, fettuccine, linguine, or spaghetti
Salt and pepper
1 tablespoon finely chopped fresh Italian parsley

In a large nonstick saucepan or skillet, heat the olive oil with the onion and garlic over moderate heat. When they sizzle, add the lamb and sauté, stirring and breaking up the meat with a wooden spoon, until the lamb begins to brown, 5 to 7 minutes.

Add the wine and stir and scrape to deglaze the pan deposits. Stir in the tomatoes, tomato paste, rosemary, sugar, and bay leaf.

Simmer the sauce until it is thick but still slightly liquid, 20 to 25 minutes.

Meanwhile, bring a large pot of water to a boil. Add the pasta and cook until al dente, following manufacturer's suggested cooking time.

When the sauce is ready, remove and discard the bay leaf and season the sauce to taste with salt and pepper. Drain the pasta and immediately toss with the sauce. Garnish with parsley.

Serves 4

NUTRITIONAL ANALYSIS PER SERVING
Calories: 493   *Total fat:* 7.34 g
Saturated fat: 2.11 g   *Cholesterol:* 56.18 mg
Sodium: 284 mg

Diced Canadian Bacon with Lentils

This rustic, brothy dish is incredibly satisfying when served over pasta shapes cooked to a good, chewy al dente texture. Leave out the Canadian bacon and substitute vegetable broth for a vegetarian version.

1 tablespoon olive oil
6 medium garlic cloves, thinly sliced
4 cups concentrated fat-free chicken broth (see page 4)
1 cup brown lentils
½ pound Canadian bacon, trimmed and cut into ½-inch cubes
2 medium carrots, cut into ¼-inch-thick slices
2 medium leeks, cut lengthwise into halves, thoroughly washed,
    and cut crosswise into ¼-inch-thick slices
1 medium onion, coarsely chopped
1 bay leaf
¾ pound dried farfalle or other medium-sized pasta shapes
6 tablespoons coarsely chopped fresh Italian parsley
Salt and pepper
1 lemon, cut into 4 wedges

In a large nonstick saucepan, heat the olive oil over moderate heat. Add the garlic and sauté 2 to 3 minutes. Add the concentrated chicken broth, lentils, Canadian bacon, carrots, leeks, onion, and bay leaf. Bring to a boil, then reduce the heat and simmer gently, partially covered, until the lentils are tender, 50 minutes to 1 hour.

Meanwhile, bring a large pot of water to a boil. Add the pasta and cook until al dente, following manufacturer's suggested cooking time.

Remove and discard the bay leaf from the bacon-lentil mixture. Stir in the parsley and season to taste with salt and pepper. Drain the pasta and ladle the bacon-lentil mixture on top. Serve with lemon wedges to squeeze to taste.

Serves 4

NUTRITIONAL ANALYSIS PER SERVING
Calories: 748   *Total fat:* 9.54 g
Saturated fat: 2.00 g   *Cholesterol:* 28 mg
Sodium: 989 mg

Canadian Bolognese

Lean Canadian bacon adds its intriguingly smoky, slightly sweet flavor to this Bolognese-style sauce featuring ground pork tenderloin.

1 tablespoon olive oil
2 medium shallots, finely chopped
1 small onion, finely chopped
*½ pound pork tenderloin, trimmed of all visible fat
    and chopped in a food processor (see page 6)*
*¼ pound Canadian bacon, trimmed and chopped
    in a food processor (see page 6)*
½ cup medium-dry white wine
1 16-ounce can crushed tomatoes
1 tablespoon tomato paste
1 tablespoon finely chopped fresh basil leaves
1 teaspoon sugar
1 teaspoon dried oregano
½ teaspoon dried rosemary
1 bay leaf
¾ pound dried spaghetti or linguine
Salt and pepper
1 tablespoon finely chopped fresh Italian parsley

Bring a large pot of water to a boil.

Meanwhile, in a large nonstick saucepan or skillet, heat the olive oil with the shallots and onion over moderate heat. When they sizzle, add the pork and Canadian bacon and sauté, stirring and breaking up the meat with a wooden spoon, until the meat begins to brown, about 7 minutes.

Add the wine and stir and scrape to deglaze the pan deposits. Stir in the tomatoes, tomato paste, basil, sugar, oregano, rosemary, and bay leaf. Simmer the sauce until thick but still slightly liquid, 20 to 25 minutes.

While the sauce is simmering, add the pasta to the boiling water and cook until al dente, following manufacturer's suggested cooking time.

When the sauce is ready, remove and discard the bay leaf. Season the sauce to taste with salt and pepper. Drain the pasta and immediately toss with the sauce. Garnish with parsley.

Serves 4

NUTRITIONAL ANALYSIS PER SERVING
Calories: 526   *Total fat:* 9.03 g
Saturated fat: 1.96 g *Cholesterol:* 51 mg
Sodium: 655 mg

Stir-Fried Pork Tenderloin with Shiitake Mushrooms and Scallions

The lightness, even delicacy, of today's pork is highlighted by this Asian-style preparation. You'll find dried shiitake mushrooms and mirin in Asian stores or the Asian food sections of most well-stocked supermarkets.

2 ounces dried shiitake mushrooms
¾ pound dried linguine or fettuccine
½ tablespoon vegetable oil
4 medium scallions, thinly sliced
2 medium garlic cloves, finely chopped
1 tablespoon grated fresh gingerroot
¾ pound pork tenderloin, trimmed of all visible fat
     and cut into ¼-inch-thick slices
2 tablespoons low-sodium soy sauce
1 tablespoon mirin (Japanese rice wine)
½ tablespoon brown sugar
½ teaspoon Worcestershire sauce
1 cup concentrated fat-free chicken broth (see page 4)
1 tablespoon cornstarch

Put the shiitake mushrooms in a small bowl and cover with warm water. Let them soak until soft, about 15 minutes.

Meanwhile, bring a large pot of water to a boil.

Drain the mushrooms. Trim and discard their stems and cut the caps into ¼-inch-wide slices.

Add the pasta to the boiling water and cook until al dente, following manufacturer's suggested cooking time.

While the pasta cooks, in a nonstick wok or large skillet, heat the vegetable oil over high heat. Add the scallions, garlic, and gingerroot and, as soon as they give off their aromas, add the pork and the shiitake mushrooms and stir-fry until the meat begins to brown, 3 to 4 minutes. Add the soy sauce, mirin, brown sugar, and Worcestershire sauce and stir well.

Add ¾ cup of the concentrated chicken broth to the wok. Stir the cornstarch into the remaining broth until dissolved and, as soon as the liquid in the wok begins to simmer, reduce the heat to moderate and stir in the cornstarch mixture. Continue simmering just until the liquid thickens to coating consistency, 1 to 2 minutes.

Drain the pasta and top with the pork and sauce.

Serves 4

NUTRITIONAL ANALYSIS PER SERVING
Calories: 530   *Total fat:* 6.11 g
Saturated fat: 1.43 g   *Cholesterol:* 55 mg
Sodium: 398 mg

New Mexican Green Chili Pork and Tomatoes

Starting with New Mexico's traditional stew of mild green chili peppers and pork, this recipe transforms the dish into a pasta sauce with the addition of tomatoes.

> 1 tablespoon olive oil
> 1 pound pork tenderloin, trimmed of all visible fat
>   and cut into 1- by ½-inch chunks
> Salt and pepper
> 4 medium garlic cloves, finely chopped
> 10 fresh long green chili peppers, roasted, stemmed,
>   and peeled (see page 7), and coarsely chopped with seeds
> 1 16-ounce can crushed tomatoes
> 1 cup concentrated fat-free chicken broth (see page 4)
> ¾ pound dried ruote or farfalle
> ¼ cup finely chopped fresh cilantro

In a large nonstick saucepan, heat the olive oil over moderate-to-high heat. Season the pork to taste with salt and pepper and sauté until it is evenly browned, about 5 minutes. Remove from the pan and pour off all but the thinnest film of fat.

Add the garlic and, as soon as it sizzles, return the pork to the pan with the chilies, tomatoes, and concentrated chicken broth. Bring the mixture to a boil, then reduce the heat and simmer, partially covered, until the pork is tender and the sauce is thick but still slightly liquid, about 45 minutes.

Meanwhile, bring a large pot of water to a boil. Add the pasta and cook until al dente, following manufacturer's suggested cooking time.

When the sauce is ready, adjust the seasoning to taste with salt and pepper. Drain the pasta and immediately toss with the sauce. Garnish with cilantro.

Serves 4

NUTRITIONAL ANALYSIS PER SERVING
Calories: 563   *Total fat:* 9.08 g
Saturated fat: 2.03 g   *Cholesterol:* 74 mg
Sodium: 275 mg

Lean Pork Meatballs with Fresh Tomato Sauce

Delicate pork meatballs are paired here with a sauce of fresh tomatoes quickly prepared at the same time the meatballs and pasta cook—a satisfying dish you can have on the table in well under half an hour.

¾ pound pork tenderloin, trimmed of all visible fat
    and chopped in a food processor (see page 6)
1 slice fresh white bread, crusts trimmed off and discarded,
    finely crumbled
2 egg whites
2 tablespoons nonfat milk
2 tablespoons finely chopped fresh chives
2 tablespoons finely chopped fresh Italian parsley
1 teaspoon dried oregano, finely crumbled
Salt and pepper
Nonstick cooking spray
¾ pound dried spaghetti or linguine
½ tablespoon olive oil
4 medium shallots, finely chopped
1¼ pounds firm ripe Roma tomatoes, cored and coarsely chopped
2 tablespoons finely shredded fresh basil

Bring a large pot of water to a boil.

In a mixing bowl, use your hands to thoroughly mix together the pork, bread crumbs, egg whites, milk, 1 tablespoon each of the chives and parsley, the oregano, and salt and pepper to taste.

Remove the broiler tray, spray it lightly with nonstick cooking spray, and set it aside. Preheat the broiler.

Using a tablespoon and your fingers, scoop and shape rounded tablespoons of the pork mixture, forming balls and placing them on the broiler tray. Broil close to the heat until golden brown, turning the meatballs once, about 5 minutes per side.

As soon as the meatballs start broiling, add the pasta to the boiling water and cook until al dente, following manufacturer's suggested cooking time.

While the meatballs and pasta cook, in a large nonstick skillet, heat the olive oil with the shallots over moderate heat. When the shallots sizzle, add the tomatoes and basil and the remaining chives and parsley. Season to taste with salt and pepper. Sauté, stirring frequently, until the tomatoes reduce to a thick but still slightly liquid sauce, 5 to 7 minutes.

Drain the pasta and immediately toss with the sauce. Arrange the meatballs on top.

Serves 4

NUTRITIONAL ANALYSIS PER SERVING
Calories: 498   *Total fat:* 6.85 g
Saturated fat: 1.51 g   *Cholesterol:* 56 mg
Sodium: 124 mg

Grilled Pork Tenderloin with Barbecue-Tomato Sauce

If you're craving a main course with some real down-home flavor, try this surprisingly elegant-looking preparation: pasta tossed with a tangy barbecue sauce, with slices of charred, lean pork tenderloin draped on top.

3 tablespoons molasses
1 tablespoon orange juice
1 pound pork tenderloin, trimmed of all visible fat
½ tablespoon vegetable oil
1 medium green bell pepper, halved, stemmed, seeded
    (see page 7), and cut into ½-inch dice
1 small red onion, coarsely chopped
2 medium garlic cloves, finely chopped
1 16-ounce can crushed tomatoes
1½ tablespoons dark brown sugar
1 tablespoon tomato paste
1 tablespoon cider vinegar
1 tablespoon finely chopped fresh parsley
½ tablespoon dried oregano
1 bay leaf
Salt and pepper
¾ pound dried spaghetti or linguine
1 tablespoon finely chopped fresh cilantro or chives

In a shallow bowl, stir together 1 tablespoon of the molasses with the orange juice. Add the pork and turn the pork in the mixture to coat evenly. Marinate at room temperature, turning occasionally, for 30 minutes.

Meanwhile, bring a large pot of water to a boil. Preheat the broiler or grill until very hot.

Also at the same time, in a large nonstick skillet or saucepan, heat the vegetable oil over moderate heat. Add the bell pepper, onion, and garlic and sauté about 2 minutes. Stir in the tomatoes, brown sugar, tomato paste, cider vinegar, parsley, oregano, bay leaf, and the remaining molasses. Simmer briskly until thick but still slightly liquid, 10 to 15 minutes.

At the same time as the sauce is simmering, remove the pork from the marinade and season to taste with salt and pepper. Broil or grill until well charred and cooked through, about 6 minutes per side.

While the pork grills, add the pasta to the boiling water and cook until al dente, following manufacturer's suggested cooking time.

When the sauce is ready, remove and discard the bay leaf and season the sauce to taste with salt and pepper. Drain the pasta and immediately toss with the sauce. Cut the pork into ¼-inch-thick slices and drape the pork on top of the pasta. Garnish with cilantro or chives.

Serves 4

NUTRITIONAL ANALYSIS PER SERVING
Calories: 577   *Total fat:* 7.35 g
Saturated fat: 7.35 g   *Cholesterol:* 74 mg
Sodium: 292 mg

❧

Pork Fajita Stir-Fry

This quick cooking method of the Southwest complements the naturally sweet, meaty flavor of lean pork. The tomatoes help form a rapid sauce that makes them an excellent topping for pasta.

1 tablespoon olive oil
½ tablespoon lemon juice
½ tablespoon orange juice
1 teaspoon dried oregano
½ teaspoon ground cumin
½ teaspoon pure red chili powder
2 medium garlic cloves, finely chopped
1 small hot green or red chili, seeded and finely chopped
1 pound pork tenderloin, trimmed of all visible fat and
    cut into strips 1 to 2 inches long and ½-inch-wide and thick
Nonstick cooking spray, preferably olive oil-flavored
1 medium red onion, halved and thinly sliced
1 medium green or red bell pepper, quartered, stemmed,
    and seeded, quarters cut crosswise into ¼-inch-wide strips
1 long mild green chili, cut lengthwise into halves, stemmed,
    and seeded, halves cut crosswise into ¼-inch-wide strips
¾ pound dried fettuccine, tagliatelle, or papardelle
1 pound firm, ripe Roma tomatoes, cored and coarsely chopped
1 teaspoon sugar
Salt and white pepper
2 tablespoons finely chopped fresh cilantro leaves

In a mixing bowl, stir together the olive oil, lemon and orange juices, oregano, cumin, chili powder, garlic, and small green or red chili. Add the pork strips and turn the pork in the mixture to coat. Marinate at room temperature for about 30 minutes.

Spray a large nonstick skillet or wok with nonstick cooking spray and heat over high heat. Add the pork mixture, onion, bell pepper, and mild green chili; cook, stirring constantly, until the pork is evenly seared and lightly browned along its edges, about 5 minutes.

Meanwhile, bring a large pot of water to a boil. Add the pasta and cook until al dente, following manufacturer's suggested cooking time.

While the pasta cooks, add the tomatoes and sugar to the pork mixture and continue cooking and stirring over high heat until the tomatoes give up their juices and form a thick but still slightly liquid sauce around the pork and vegetables, about 5 minutes more. Season to taste with salt and white pepper.

Drain the pasta and immediately top with the sauce. Garnish with cilantro.

Serves 4

NUTRITIONAL ANALYSIS PER SERVING
Calories: 544   *Total fat:* 9.40 g
Saturated fat: 2.02 g *Cholesterol:* 74 mg
Sodium: 82 mg

7

Dairy

Low-Fat Three-Cheese Sauce

Romano-and-Herb Toss

Smoked Gouda Cream Sauce

Egg-White Carbonara with Mushrooms

Breakfast Pasta with Egg Whites, Tomatoes, and Garlic

Breakfast Pasta with Egg Whites, Smoked Salmon,
Cream Cheese, and Dillweed

Light Macaroni and Cheese

Sweet Spiced Ricotta and Applesauce Melt

Light Cheese Lasagna

Stuffed Shells with Herbed Ricotta

Low-Fat Three-Cheese Sauce

I included a low-fat sauce similar to this one in the first volume of Pasta Light. *But the improved melting qualities of fat-free cheeses make it possible to do even better now in the health category.*

1½ cups evaporated skimmed milk
2 teaspoons cornstarch
¾ pound dried fettuccine or tagliatelle
2 ounces fat-free cheddar cheese, finely shredded
2 ounces fat-free Swiss cheese, finely shredded
2 ounces fat-free cream cheese, at room temperature
2 tablespoons grated Romano cheese
Pepper
1 tablespoon finely chopped fresh Italian parsley

In a small cup or bowl, pour ½ cup of the evaporated milk. Sprinkle and stir in the cornstarch until dissolved and set aside.

Bring a large pot of water to a boil. Add the pasta and cook until al dente, following manufacturer's suggested cooking time.

Meanwhile, in a medium saucepan or skillet, bring the remaining 1 cup of evaporated milk to a simmer over moderate heat. Sprinkle and stir in the cheddar and Swiss cheeses. In small pieces, drop in the cream cheese. When the cheeses begin to melt, briefly restir the milk-cornstarch mixture and add to the cheese mixture, along with the Romano cheese. Continue stirring until the sauce is thick and creamy. Season to taste with pepper.

Drain the pasta and immediately toss with the sauce. Garnish with parsley.

Serves 4

NUTRITIONAL ANALYSIS PER SERVING
Calories: 458   *Total fat:* 2.20 g
Saturated fat: .30 g   *Cholesterol:* 9 mg
Sodium: 469 mg

Romano-and-Herb Toss

This dish is at once flavorful and colorful, yet simple and light.

> *¾ pound dried spaghetti or linguine*
> *1 packet (½ ounce) Butter Buds brand natural butter flavoring*
> *½ cup hot tap water*
> *½ cup grated Romano cheese*
> *2 tablespoons finely chopped fresh Italian parsley*
> *2 tablespoons finely chopped fresh basil leaves*
> *2 tablespoons finely chopped fresh chives*
> *Pepper*

Bring a large pot of water to a boil. Add the pasta and cook until al dente. Meanwhile, in a measuring cup or bowl, stir the Butter Buds into the ½ cup of hot water until completely dissolved. Set aside.

In a mixing bowl, toss together the Romano cheese, parsley, basil, and chives. Set aside. As soon as the pasta is ready, drain it and transfer it to a large serving bowl. Add the liquified Butter Buds and the Romano-herb mixture and toss well. Season to taste with pepper.

Serves 4

NUTRITIONAL ANALYSIS PER SERVING
Calories: 369   *Total fat:* 4.05 g
Saturated fat: .19 g   *Cholesterol:* 11 mg
Sodium: 297 mg

❧

Smoked Gouda Cream Sauce

I've made the delightful discovery that smoked Gouda cheese, rich and flavorful though it tastes, can be remarkably low in fat—in fact, as low as 16 percent or so calories from fat. Read labels and seek it out to use in this satisfying sauce.

¾ pound dried rigatoni or other medium-sized to
  large tubes or shapes
1 cup evaporated skimmed milk
½ pound smoked Gouda cheese, shredded
1 teaspoon creamy Dijon mustard
1 tablespoon finely chopped fresh chives

Bring a large pot of water to a boil. Add the pasta and cook until al dente. When the pasta is almost cooked, in a medium saucepan or skillet, bring the evaporated milk to a simmer over moderate heat. Gradually sprinkle and stir in the cheese. As the cheese begins to melt, stir in the mustard and continue stirring until the sauce is creamy.

Drain the pasta and immediately toss with the sauce. Garnish with chives.

Serves 4

NUTRITIONAL ANALYSIS PER SERVING
Calories: 569   *Total fat:* 17.03 g
Saturated fat: 10.25 g   *Cholesterol:* 67 mg
Sodium: 574 mg

Egg-White Carbonara with Mushrooms

Egg whites replace the whole eggs and meaty-tasting mushrooms replace the ham in this lightened version of Italian "charcoal maker's" pasta.

> ¾ pound dried spaghetti or linguine
> 12 egg whites, lightly beaten
> ½ cup grated Romano cheese
> 1 tablespoon finely chopped fresh chives
> 1 tablespoon finely chopped fresh basil leaves
> Butter-flavored nonstick cooking spray
> 2 medium shallots, finely chopped
> ¼ pound fresh cremini or white mushrooms, stems trimmed,
>   caps cut into ¼-inch-thick slices
> Black pepper

Bring a large pot of water to a boil. Add the pasta and cook until al dente, following manufacturer's suggested cooking time.

Meanwhile, in a mixing bowl, stir together the egg whites, Romano cheese, chives, and basil. Set aside.

A few minutes before the pasta is ready, heat a large nonstick skillet over high heat. Spray generously with nonstick cooking spray and add the shallots. As soon as they sizzle, add the mushrooms and sauté until they just begin to brown on their edges, 2 to 3 minutes. Reduce the heat to low.

Drain the pasta and add it to the skillet with the egg mixture. Stir and toss continuously until the sauce thickens and coats the pasta, 2 to 3 minutes. Season to taste with black pepper.

Serves 4

NUTRITIONAL ANALYSIS PER SERVING
Calories: 419   *Total fat:* 4.65 g
Saturated fat: .20 g   *Cholesterol:* 10 mg
Sodium: 292 mg

Breakfast Pasta with Egg Whites, Tomatoes, and Garlic

For those who like a robust breakfast, this aromatic mixture will start the day off right without adding much in the way of fat. If you'd like a tamer dish, reduce or leave out the garlic.

¾ pound dried spaghetti or linguine
½ tablespoon olive oil
4 medium garlic cloves, finely chopped
6 medium Roma tomatoes, cored, halved, seeded (see page 8),
   and coarsely chopped
12 egg whites, lightly beaten
½ cup grated Romano cheese
2 tablespoons finely chopped fresh Italian parsley
Pepper

Bring a large pot of water to a boil. Add the pasta and cook until al dente, following manufacturer's suggested cooking time.

While the pasta is cooking, in a large nonstick skillet, heat the olive oil with the garlic over moderate heat. As soon as the garlic sizzles, add the tomatoes and sauté about 1 minute, just until heated through. Remove from the heat.

As soon as the pasta is cooked, drain it and add it to the skillet over low heat. Add the egg whites, Romano cheese, and parsley and stir and toss continuously until the sauce thickens and coats the pasta, 2 to 3 minutes. Season to taste with pepper.

Serves 4

NUTRITIONAL ANALYSIS PER SERVING
Calories: 437   *Total fat:* 5.91 g
Saturated fat: .44 g   *Cholesterol:* 10 mg
Sodium: 297 mg

Breakfast Pasta with Egg Whites, Smoked Salmon, Cream Cheese, and Dillweed

A deli-style twist on a uniquely Italian approach to eating pasta.

> ¾ *pound dried spaghetti or linguine*
> ½ *tablespoon butter*
> 2 *medium shallots, finely chopped*
> 12 *egg whites, lightly beaten*
> 6 *ounces smoked salmon, cut into ¼- by 1-inch strips*
> ¼ *cup grated Romano cheese*
> ¼ *pound fat-free cream cheese, at room temperature*
> *Pepper*
> 2 *tablespoons finely chopped fresh dillweed*

Bring a large pot of water to a boil. Add the pasta and cook until al dente, following manufacturer's suggested cooking time.

Just before the pasta is cooked, in a large nonstick skillet, melt the butter with the shallots over moderate heat. As soon as the shallots sizzle, reduce the heat to low, drain the pasta, and add it to the skillet. Add the egg whites, smoked salmon, and Romano cheese and cook until the sauce begins to thicken and coat the pasta, 1 to 2 minutes.

With your fingers, quickly pinch off small pieces of the cream cheese and dot them all over the pasta; continue cooking, stirring gently, until the cream cheese melts and the sauce is thick, 1 to 2 minutes more. Season to taste with pepper. Garnish with dillweed.

Serves 4

NUTRITIONAL ANALYSIS PER SERVING
Calories: 477   *Total fat:* 5.95 g
Saturated fat: 1.47 g   *Cholesterol:* 22 mg
Sodium: 715 mg

Light Macaroni and Cheese

A couple of simple tricks—nonfat cheese and a cornstarch-thickened sauce—produce a dish as satisfying as any that came from Grandma's kitchen. Try substituting other nonfat cheeses with good melting qualities for some of the cheddar.

¾ pound dried macaroni or small to medium-sized shells
1½ cups evaporated skimmed milk
2 teaspoons cornstarch
¾ pound nonfat sharp cheddar cheese, finely shredded
Salt and pepper
Butter-flavored or plain nonstick cooking spray

Preheat the broiler.

Bring a large pot of water to a boil. Add the pasta and cook until al dente, following manufacturer's suggested cooking time.

Meanwhile, in a medium saucepan, bring 1 cup of the evaporated milk to a simmer over low-to-moderate heat. In a small cup or bowl, sprinkle and stir the cornstarch into the remaining milk until dissolved. Gradually pour and stir the cornstarch-milk mixture into the hot milk; then sprinkle and stir in ½ pound of the shredded cheddar cheese. Continue stirring until the cheese melts and the sauce is thick. Season to taste with salt and pepper.

When the pasta is cooked, drain it thoroughly and immediately toss with the cheese sauce. Spray a baking dish with the nonstick spray and transfer the macaroni and cheese to the dish. Sprinkle the remaining cheese on top and broil until the cheese melts and bubbles, 3 to 5 minutes.

Serves 4

NUTRITIONAL ANALYSIS PER SERVING
Calories: 517   *Total fat:* 1.78 g
Saturated fat: .30 g   *Cholesterol:* 12 mg
Sodium: 987 mg

Sweet Spiced Ricotta and Applesauce Melt

In this grown-up interpretation of nursery food, just-warmed ricotta is seasoned with sweet baking spices and applesauce and gently melted in buttery-tasting liquid.

¾ pound dried farfalle or other medium-sized pasta shapes
15 ounces fat-free ricotta cheese, at room temperature
½ cup unsweetened applesauce
1 tablespoon dark brown sugar
1 teaspoon powdered cinnamon
⅛ teaspoon ground allspice
Pinch of grated nutmeg
Pinch of ground cloves
2 packets (1 ounce) Butter Buds brand natural butter flavoring
1 cup hot tap water

Bring a large pot of water to a boil. Add the pasta and cook until al dente, following manufacturer's suggested cooking time.

Meanwhile, in a mixing bowl, stir and mash together the ricotta cheese, applesauce, brown sugar, cinnamon, allspice, nutmeg, and cloves until smoothly blended.

In a small mixing bowl, stir the Butter Buds into the cup of hot water until completely dissolved.

Drain the pasta and immediately spoon small clumps of the ricotta mixture all over its surface. Drizzle the hot liquified Butter Buds on top and serve immediately.

Serves 4

NUTRITIONAL ANALYSIS PER SERVING
Calories: 455   *Total fat:* 1.37 g
Saturated fat: .19 g   *Cholesterol:* 1 mg
Sodium: 565 mg

Light Cheese Lasagna

This recipe yields for each person what my wife refers to as a "generous slab of lasagna." Filling and satisfying though it is, I've lightened it by using nonfat ricotta and mozzarella cheeses.

1 tablespoon olive oil
1 small onion, finely chopped
1 medium garlic clove, finely chopped
1 16-ounce can crushed tomatoes
2 tablespoons tomato paste
1 tablespoon sugar
2 teaspoons dried oregano
1 bay leaf
⅓ pound dried lasagna noodles
½ cup evaporated skimmed milk
2 tablespoons finely shredded fresh basil leaves
2 tablespoons finely chopped fresh Italian parsley
Salt and pepper
15 ounces fat-free ricotta cheese
¼ cup grated Romano cheese
2 egg whites, lightly beaten
Pinch of nutmeg
Nonstick cooking spray
½ pound fat-free mozzarella or Monterey Jack cheese,
    coarsely shredded

Bring a large pot of water to a boil. Meanwhile, in a large nonstick skillet or saucepan, heat the olive oil over moderate heat. Add the onion and garlic and sauté until they begin to turn transparent, 2 to 3 minutes. Add the tomatoes, tomato paste, sugar, oregano, and bay leaf and simmer briskly until thick, 10 to 15 minutes.

While the sauce is cooking, add the pasta to the boiling water and cook until al dente. Drain. When the sauce is ready, remove and discard the bay leaf and stir in the evaporated milk, basil, and parsley. Season to taste with salt and pepper and set aside.

In a mixing bowl, stir together the ricotta and Romano cheeses, egg whites, and nutmeg until smooth.

Preheat the oven to 375°F. Lightly spray a deep 8-inch-square baking dish with nonstick cooking spray. Spoon a thin layer of the tomato sauce on the bottom. Arrange one-third of the cooked pasta on top, trimming the noodles to fit. Spread one-third of the sauce on the noodles, then a third of the ricotta mixture, and a third of the mozzarella. Repeat in that order until all the ingredients are used, ending with the mozzarella.

Cover the dish loosely with foil, not touching the mozzarella, and bake for about 30 minutes. Remove the foil and bake 20 to 30 minutes more, until the lasagna is bubbly and the top is golden. Remove from the oven and let the lasagna settle for 5 to 10 minutes before slicing and serving.

Serves 4

NUTRITIONAL ANALYSIS PER SERVING
Calories: 466   *Total fat:* 6.11 g
Saturated fat: .62 g   *Cholesterol:* 12 mg
Sodium: 1,070 mg

Stuffed Shells with Herbed Ricotta

There's something especially pleasurable about cutting into a stuffed, baked pasta shell, especially when the shell is stuffed with a filling as fluffy, colorful, and flavorful as the one in this recipe. If you like, you also can top the shells before baking with a simple tomato sauce like the one prepared in the Light Cheese Lasagna recipe (see page 148).

2 dozen dried large pasta shells for stuffing
15 ounces fat-free ricotta cheese
½ cup grated Romano cheese
4 egg whites, lightly beaten
3 tablespoons finely chopped fresh chives
3 tablespoons finely shredded fresh basil leaves
2 tablespoons finely chopped fresh Italian parsley
Salt and pepper
Butter-flavored nonstick cooking spray
¼ pound nonfat mozzarella cheese, shredded
½ cup evaporated skimmed milk

Preheat the oven to 375°F.

Bring a large pot of water to a boil. Add the pasta and cook until al dente, following manufacturer's suggested cooking time. Drain well.

In a mixing bowl, stir together the ricotta and Romano cheeses, egg whites, chives, basil, parsley, and salt and pepper to taste.

With the nonstick cooking spray, spray a shallow baking dish large enough to hold the shells in a single layer. Spoon the ricotta filling into the shells and place the shells, open side up, in the dish. Dot with any remaining filling, sprinkle with the mozzarella cheese, and drizzle with the evaporated milk.

Bake until the shells are bubbling and golden brown, about 30 minutes.

Serves 4

NUTRITIONAL ANALYSIS PER SERVING
Calories: 466   *Total fat:* 4.33 g
Saturated fat: .18 g   *Cholesterol:* 17 mg
Sodium: 589 mg

8

Pasta Salads

Bay Shrimp Pasta Salad with Black-Bean Salsa

Classic Tuna Pasta Salad

Waldorf-Style Tuna Pasta Salad

Asian Crab Pasta Salad with Red Peppers,
Snow Peas, and Miso Mayonnaise

Smoked Chicken Pasta Salad with
Sun-Dried Tomato-and-Basil Pesto

Asian Chicken Pasta Salad

Southwestern Turkey Pasta Salad

Smoked Turkey Pasta Salad with
Smoked Gouda, Apple, and Walnuts

Pasta Chef's Salad

Primavera Pasta Salad with Yogurt-Lemon-Herb Dressing

Grilled Ratatouille Pasta Salad

Tricolore Pasta Salad

Fresh Roma Tomato Pasta Salad

Bay Shrimp Pasta Salad with Black-Bean Salsa

Adding the bay shrimp at the last minute helps preserve their pristine color. You can make the salsa spicier or milder if you wish by increasing or decreasing the amount of chili pepper. Even without the shrimp, the combination of beans and pasta provides a complete source of protein.

¾ pound Roma tomatoes, cored and cut into ¼- to ½-inch dice
1 cup canned cooked black beans, rinsed and drained
¼ cup packed finely chopped fresh cilantro
1 medium red onion, finely chopped
1 jalapeño chili pepper, halved, stemmed, seeded, and
    finely chopped
1 small red serrano chili pepper, halved, stemmed, seeded,
    and finely chopped
1 small garlic clove, finely chopped
3 tablespoons lime juice
1 tablespoon olive oil
1 tablespoon sugar
Salt and pepper
¾ pound dried small shells or other small to medium-sized
    pasta shapes
16 Bibb lettuce leaves
¾ pound cooked baby bay shrimp
Small sprigs cilantro or parsley

In a mixing bowl, stir together the tomatoes, black beans, cilantro, onion, chilies, garlic, lime juice, olive oil, and sugar. Season to taste with salt and pepper. Cover and refrigerate for at least 1 hour.

Meanwhile, bring a large pot of water to a boil. Add the pasta and cook until al dente, following manufacturer's suggested cooking time. Drain well. Rinse under cold running water until the pasta is cold, then drain well again. Transfer to a bowl, cover, and refrigerate until serving time.

Just before serving, taste the black-bean salsa and adjust the seasoning to taste, if necessary. In a mixing bowl, toss together the salsa and pasta. Arrange on top of the lettuce leaves and scatter the shrimp on top. Garnish with cilantro or parsley sprigs.

Serves 4

NUTRITIONAL ANALYSIS PER SERVING
Calories: 532   *Total fat:* 6.38 g
Saturated fat: .95 g   *Cholesterol:* 166 mg
Sodium: 344 mg

Classic Tuna Pasta Salad

The basic elements of everyone's favorite childhood tuna sandwich, lightened with fat-free mayonnaise, are perfectly satisfying when mixed with pasta shapes to produce a lunchtime salad. Try this with canned salmon, too.

> 2 6-ounce cans white tuna in spring water, drained
> 1 medium celery rib, cut lengthwise into halves,
>   then cut crosswise into thin slices
> 1 cup fat-free mayonnaise
> 2 tablespoons lemon juice
> 1 teaspoon celery seed
> Salt and pepper
> ¾ pound dried small shells or other small to
>   medium-sized pasta shapes
> 16 small iceberg or Bibb lettuce leaves
> 2 tablespoons finely chopped fresh Italian parsley

In a mixing bowl, use a fork to mash together the tuna, celery, mayonnaise, lemon juice, and celery seed until evenly mixed, with the tuna in small flakes. Season to taste with salt and pepper.

Bring a large pot of water to a boil. Add the pasta and cook until al dente, following manufacturer's suggested cooking time. Drain well. Rinse under cold running water until the pasta is cold, then drain well again.

In a mixing bowl, toss together the pasta and the tuna mixture. Arrange on top of the lettuce leaves. Garnish with parsley.

Serves 4

Nutritional analysis per serving
Calories: 470   *Total fat:* 3.44 g
Saturated fat: .71 g   *Cholesterol:* 33 mg
Sodium: 748 mg

Waldorf-Style Tuna Pasta Salad

Tuna gains a touch of elegance when combined with some of the definitive ingredients of the salad first developed in the late nineteenth century by Oscar Tschirky, chef of New York's Waldorf Hotel. Though nuts are high in fat, just a few here do not significantly diminish the healthfulness of the salad, and they add wonderful highlights of flavor and texture.

2 large, crisp, tart apples, cored, cut into wedges,
    and then cut crosswise into ½-inch pieces
2 6-ounce cans white tuna in spring water, drained
    and flaked into ½-inch chunks
2 medium celery ribs, cut crosswise into ¼-inch-thick slices
1 cup fat-free mayonnaise
¼ cup coarsely chopped walnuts, toasted (see page 7)
2 tablespoons lemon juice
2 tablespoons finely chopped fresh chives
Salt and pepper
¾ pound dried bow ties, radiatore, or other
    medium-sized pasta shapes
12 medium romaine lettuce leaves
Italian parsley sprigs

In a mixing bowl, stir together the apples, tuna, celery, mayonnaise, walnuts, lemon juice, and chives until evenly mixed. Season to taste with salt and pepper.

Bring a large pot of water to a boil. Add the pasta and cook until al dente, following manufacturer's suggested cooking time. Drain well. Rinse under cold running water until the pasta is cold, then drain well again.

In a mixing bowl, toss together the pasta and the tuna mixture. Arrange on top of the lettuce leaves. Garnish with parsley.

Serves 4

NUTRITIONAL ANALYSIS PER SERVING
Calories: 573   *Total fat:* 8.33 g
Saturated fat: 1.16 g   *Cholesterol:* 33 mg
Sodium: 758 mg

Asian Crab Pasta Salad with Red Peppers, Snow Peas, and Miso Mayonnaise

A little Japanese miso (soybean paste) gives rich, intriguing flavor to this seafood pasta salad. Avoid using the imitation crabmeat widely available today, which can be very high in sodium and which does not match the real thing in taste or texture. If you like, make this salad with baby bay shrimp in place of the crab.

¾ pound small snow peas, trimmed
¾ pound dried small or medium-sized shells or other
  small to medium-sized pasta shapes
¾ pound cooked crabmeat, flaked and picked clean
  of shell and cartilage
1 medium red bell pepper, quartered, stemmed, seeded,
  and cut crosswise into ¼-inch-wide strips
1 cup fat-free mayonnaise
2 tablespoons Japanese yellow miso (soybean paste)
2 teaspoons honey
1 teaspoon lemon juice
¼ cup finely chopped fresh cilantro or fresh Italian parsley leaves
¼ cup finely chopped fresh chives
Salt and pepper
16 small butter lettuce leaves

Bring a large pot of water to a boil. Add the snow peas and parboil them for about 1 minute. Remove them with a wire skimmer or slotted spoon and rinse immediately under cold running water. Drain well and set aside.

Add the pasta to the boiling water and cook until al dente, following manufacturer's suggested cooking time.

Meanwhile, reserve four attractive snow peas. Cut the remaining snow peas diagonally into ¼-inch-wide pieces. Put them in a mixing bowl with the crabmeat. Add the bell pepper, reserving a few strips.

In a small bowl, stir together the mayonnaise, miso, honey, and lemon juice until smoothly blended. Add to the crabmeat mixture along with the cilantro or parsley and the chives.

When the pasta is cooked, drain well. Rinse under cold running water until the pasta is cold, then drain well again.

Add the pasta to the crabmeat mixture and thoroughly toss together all the ingredients. Season to taste with salt and pepper.

Arrange the pasta salad on top of the lettuce leaves and garnish with the reserved snow peas and pepper strips.

Serves 4

NUTRITIONAL ANALYSIS PER SERVING
Calories: 515   *Total fat:* 3.60 g
Saturated fat: .48 g   *Cholesterol:* 85 mg
Sodium: 983 mg

Smoked Chicken Pasta Salad with Sun-Dried Tomato-and-Basil Pesto

You also can try this salad with smoked turkey, if you like. The intense flavor of the dressing nicely highlights the smoky sweetness of the poultry.

¾ pound dried linguine or fettuccine

1½ cups packed stemmed fresh basil leaves

½ cup concentrated fat-free chicken broth (see page 4), chilled

¼ cup dry-packed sun-dried tomatoes, cut into ¼-inch strips

2 tablespoons grated Romano cheese

2 tablespoons pine nuts, toasted (see page 7)

2 tablespoons olive oil

1 tablespoon lemon juice

1 medium garlic clove

Salt and pepper

¾ pound smoked chicken, skin removed and discarded,
    cut into ½-inch pieces

¼ pound fat-free Monterey Jack cheese, cut into thin
    ¼- by 1-inch strips

2 medium red bell peppers, quartered, stemmed, seeded,
    and cut crosswise into ¼-inch-wide strips

16 medium Bibb or butter lettuce leaves

Whole basil leaves

Bring a large pot of water to a boil. Add the pasta and cook until al dente, following manufacturer's suggested cooking time. Drain well. Rinse under cold running water until the pasta is cold, then drain well again.

Put the stemmed basil leaves, concentrated chicken broth, sun-dried tomatoes, Romano cheese, pine nuts, olive oil, lemon juice, and garlic in a food processor fitted with the metal blade. Pulse the ingredients until they are coarsely chopped, then scrape down the work bowl and process until the mixture is smoothly pureed, adding a little cold water if necessary to achieve a thick but slightly fluid consistency. Season to taste with salt and pepper.

In a mixing bowl, toss together the pasta, chicken, Monterey Jack cheese, bell peppers, and pesto dressing. Arrange the salad on top of the lettuce leaves. Garnish with whole basil leaves.

Serves 4

NUTRITIONAL ANALYSIS PER SERVING
Calories: 678   *Total fat:* 18.08 g
Saturated fat: 3.21 g   *Cholesterol:* 78 mg
Sodium: 1,116 mg

Asian Chicken Pasta Salad

With its intriguing hints of sweet, sour, and rich, this salad satisfies as well as much more calorie-laden versions do. If you can't find Chinese noodles in the Asian food section of your market, regular pasta strands will do.

> ¾ pound uncooked egg-free Chinese chow mein noodles,
>   or linguine or fettuccine
> ⅓ cup orange juice
> ¼ cup Japanese yellow miso (soybean paste)
> ¼ cup fat-free mayonnaise
> 1 tablespoon Asian sesame oil
> 1 tablespoon mirin (Japanese rice wine)
> 1 teaspoon crushed red chili flakes (optional)
> ¾ pound cooked skinless chicken meat, coarsely chopped
> ¾ cup canned drained mandarin orange segments
> 1 medium red bell pepper, quartered, stemmed, seeded,
>   and cut crosswise into ¼-inch-wide slices
> 2 medium scallions, cut crosswise into thin slices
> ¼ cup cashew or peanut halves, toasted (see page 7)
> 12 medium Bibb or butter lettuce leaves
> 4 fresh cilantro sprigs

Bring a large pot of water to a boil. Add the pasta and cook until al dente, following manufacturer's suggested cooking time. Drain well. Rinse under cold running water until the pasta is cold, then drain well again.

In a small bowl, stir together the orange juice, miso, mayonnaise, sesame oil, and mirin until smoothly blended; add the chili flakes if you'd like a spicy salad.

In a mixing bowl, toss together the pasta, dressing, chicken, mandarin orange segments, bell pepper, scallions, and nuts until well mixed. Arrange on top of the lettuce leaves. Garnish with cilantro sprigs.

Serves 4

NUTRITIONAL ANALYSIS PER SERVING
Calories: 654   *Total fat:* 16.23 g
Saturated fat: 3.34 g   *Cholesterol:* 76 mg
Sodium: 821 mg

Southwestern Turkey Pasta Salad

Wagon-wheel pasta, also known as Italian ruote, seems appropriate for this hearty mixture of turkey, Monterey Jack cheese, and corn. The tomato salsa dressing gets its spice from the smoked form of jalapeño peppers, known as chipotles, which are widely available canned in the Mexican or specialty-food section of the market.

1 pound Roma tomatoes, cored and coarsely chopped
1 cup canned sweet corn, drained
1 small red onion, finely chopped
2 tablespoons finely chopped fresh basil leaves
2 tablespoons red wine vinegar
1 tablespoon olive oil
1 teaspoon dried oregano, crumbled
2 canned chipotle chili peppers, finely chopped
Salt and pepper
¾ pound dried wagon-wheels or other medium-sized
    pasta shapes
¾ pound cooked skinless turkey breast, cut into
    ½-inch pieces
6 ounces fat-free Monterey Jack cheese, cut into thin
    ¼- by 1-inch pieces
16 Bibb lettuce leaves
Whole basil leaves

In a mixing bowl, stir together the tomatoes, corn, onion, basil, red wine vinegar, olive oil, oregano, and chipotle chilies. Season to taste with salt and pepper. Cover and refrigerate for at least 1 hour.

Meanwhile, bring a large pot of water to a boil. Add the pasta and cook until al dente, following manufacturer's suggested cooking time. Drain well. Rinse under cold running water until the pasta is cold, then drain well again. Transfer to a bowl, cover, and refrigerate until serving time.

Just before serving, taste the tomato-chipotle salsa and adjust the seasoning to taste, if necessary. In a mixing bowl, toss together the salsa, pasta, turkey, and Monterey Jack cheese. Arrange on top of the lettuce leaves. Garnish with whole basil leaves.

Serves 4

NUTRITIONAL ANALYSIS PER SERVING
Calories: 620   *Total fat:* 6.62 g
Saturated fat: 1.01 g   *Cholesterol:* 71 mg
Sodium: 649 mg

☙

Smoked Turkey Pasta Salad with Smoked Gouda, Apple, and Walnuts

One of the most satisfying combinations I know of in a pasta salad is the smokiness of the turkey and cheese, the sweetness of the apple, the rich crunch of the walnuts, all highlighted by a creamy, tangy dressing. Try substituting hazelnuts for the walnuts, or smoked chicken for the turkey.

¾ pound dried medium-sized shells or other pasta shapes
1 cup fat-free mayonnaise
2 tablespoons grainy Dijon mustard
1 tablespoon finely chopped fresh Italian parsley
1 tablespoon finely chopped fresh chives
2 teaspoons cider vinegar
Salt and pepper
1 pound skinless smoked turkey breast, cut into ½-inch pieces
½ pound smoked Gouda cheese, cut into ¼-inch chunks
1 large crisp green apple, cored, peel left on, apple cut into
    ¼- to ½-inch pieces
4 large romaine or iceberg lettuce leaves
¼ cup coarsely chopped walnuts, toasted (see page 7)

Bring a large pot of water to a boil. Add the pasta and cook until al dente, following manufacturer's suggested cooking time. Drain well. Rinse under cold running water until the pasta is cold, then drain well again.

In a small bowl, stir together the mayonnaise, mustard, parsley, chives, and cider vinegar until well blended. Season to taste with salt and pepper.

In a mixing bowl, toss together the pasta, dressing, smoked turkey, Gouda cheese, and apple until well mixed. Mound on top of the lettuce leaves. Garnish with chopped walnuts.

Serves 4

NUTRITIONAL ANALYSIS PER SERVING
Calories: 774   *Total fat:* 25.79 g
Saturated fat: 12.18 g *Cholesterol:* 112 mg
Sodium: 2,139 mg

Pasta Chef's Salad

Think of your favorite chef's salad, combine it with pasta, and you'll come close to imagining this bountiful salad.

¾ pound dried medium-sized shells or other pasta shapes
1 cup fat-free mayonnaise
2 tablespoons creamy Dijon mustard
2 teaspoons lemon juice
Salt and pepper
½ pound cooked skinless turkey breast, cut into
    ¼- by 1-inch strips
½ pound extralean smoked ham, trimmed of all visible fat
    and cut into ¼- by 1-inch strips
6 ounces fat-free Swiss or cheddar cheese, cut into
    ¼- by 1-inch strips
4 medium Roma tomatoes, cored, halved, seeded (see page 8),
    and coarsely chopped
1 tablespoon finely chopped fresh Italian parsley
1 tablespoon finely chopped fresh chives
4 large iceberg lettuce leaves
Fresh parsley sprigs

Bring a large pot of water to a boil. Add the pasta and cook until al dente, following manufacturer's suggested cooking time. Drain well. Rinse under cold running water until the pasta is cold, then drain well again.

In a small bowl, stir together the mayonnaise, mustard, and lemon juice until well blended. Season to taste with salt and pepper.

In a mixing bowl, toss together the pasta, dressing, turkey, ham, Swiss or cheddar cheese, tomatoes, finely chopped parsley, and chives until well mixed. Mound on top of the lettuce leaves. Garnish with parsley sprigs.

Serves 4

NUTRITIONAL ANALYSIS PER SERVING
Calories: 589   *Total fat:* 4.77 g
Saturated fat: 1.26 g *Cholesterol:* 74 mg
Sodium: 1,783 mg

Primavera Pasta Salad with Yogurt-Lemon-Herb Dressing

Springtime's bright colors and the zesty flavors of yogurt and lemon bring this pasta salad to vivid life. Feel free to add your own favorite vegetables or fresh herbs.

½ cup low-fat plain yogurt
½ cup fat-free mayonnaise
1 tablespoon lemon juice
1 tablespoon grated lemon zest
1 tablespoon finely shredded fresh basil leaves
1 tablespoon finely chopped fresh dillweed
1 tablespoon finely chopped fresh Italian parsley
Salt and white pepper
¾ pound dried farfalle, medium-sized shells, or other pasta shapes
½ pound fresh peas, shelled (about ¾ cup)
1 medium carrot, cut into ¼-inch dice
1 medium zucchini, cut into ¼-inch dice
1 medium red bell pepper, halved, stemmed, seeded,
    and cut into ¼-inch dice

Bring a large pot of water to a boil.

Meanwhile, in a mixing bowl, stir together the yogurt, mayonnaise, lemon juice and zest, basil, dillweed, and parsley. Season to taste with salt and white pepper and set aside.

Add the pasta to the boiling water and cook until al dente, following manufacturer's suggested cooking time. About halfway through the pasta's cooking time, add the peas and carrot to the boiling water; about three-fourths of the way through the pasta's cooking time, add the zucchini.

Drain the pasta and vegetables. Rinse under cold running water until cool, then drain well again. Add to a mixing bowl with the red bell pepper. Add the dressing and toss well, adjusting the seasonings to taste. Cover and refrigerate until serving time.

Serves 4

Nutritional analysis per serving
Calories: 422   *Total fat:* 2.12 g
Saturated fat: .51 g   *Cholesterol:* 2 mg
Sodium: 248 mg

Grilled Ratatouille Pasta Salad

Here the vegetables that make up the familiar ratatouille of the south of France are grilled separately instead of stewed, then chopped and tossed with pasta to make a colorful summertime salad.

¾ pound dried farfalle, medium-sized shells,
    or other pasta shapes
2 tablespoons balsamic vinegar
1 tablespoon olive oil
2 medium Japanese eggplants, trimmed and cut lengthwise
    into ½-inch-thick slices
2 medium firm ripe tomatoes, trimmed and cut
    into ½-inch-thick slices
2 medium zucchini, trimmed and cut lengthwise
    into ½-inch-thick slices
1 large red onion, cut into ½-inch-thick slices
1 medium green bell pepper, quartered, stemmed, and seeded,
    and cut lengthwise into ½-inch-thick slices
Olive oil-flavored nonstick cooking spray
Salt and pepper
½ cup concentrated vegetable broth (see page 4)
2 tablespoons fat-free mayonnaise
1 tablespoon finely shredded fresh basil leaves
1 tablespoon finely chopped fresh Italian parsley
1 tablespoon finely chopped fresh chives

Preheat the broiler or grill until very hot.

Meanwhile, bring a large pot of water to a boil. Add the pasta and cook until al dente, following manufacturer's suggested cooking time. Drain well. Rinse with cold running water, then drain well again. Set aside.

In a small bowl, stir together the balsamic vinegar and olive oil. Use a basting brush to lightly brush the eggplant, tomato, zucchini, onion, and green bell pepper slices with the mixture.

Spray the mixture lightly with nonstick cooking spray and season to taste with salt and pepper. Broil or grill until golden brown, about 5 minutes per side. Set aside to cool, then chop coarsely.

In a small bowl, stir together the concentrated vegetable broth, mayonnaise, basil, parsley, and chives. Toss this mixture together with the pasta and chopped vegetables and adjust the seasoning to taste with salt and pepper.

Serves 4

NUTRITIONAL ANALYSIS PER SERVING
Calories: 427   *Total fat:* 5.43 g
Saturated fat: .70 g   *Cholesterol:* 0 mg
Sodium: 139 mg

Tricolore Pasta Salad

Pasta here becomes a background for the classic Italian appetizer salad of tomatoes, basil, and mozzarella—the three colors of the Italian flag. If you can't find fat-free mozzarella, substitute fat-free Monterey Jack cheese.

¾ pound dried rotelli or other medium-sized pasta shapes
6 tablespoons balsamic vinegar
2 tablespoons olive oil
1 tablespoon creamy Dijon mustard
Salt and pepper
8 medium Roma tomatoes, cored, halved, seeded (see page 8), and coarsely chopped
¾ pound fat-free mozzarella cheese, cut into ½-inch cubes
½ cup packed thinly shredded fresh basil leaves
Whole basil leaves

Bring a large pot of water to a boil. Add the pasta and cook until al dente, following manufacturer's suggested cooking time. Drain well. Rinse under cold running water until the pasta is cold, then drain well again.

In a small bowl, stir together the balsamic vinegar, olive oil, and mustard; season to taste with salt and pepper.

In a mixing bowl, toss together the pasta, dressing, tomatoes, mozzarella cheese, and shredded basil. Adjust the seasoning to taste. Garnish with whole basil leaves.

Serves 4

NUTRITIONAL ANALYSIS PER SERVING
Calories: 526   *Total fat:* 8.45 g
Saturated fat: 1.13 g *Cholesterol:* 15 mg
Sodium: 825 mg

Fresh Roma Tomato Pasta Salad

Always reliable, Roma tomatoes let you bring the taste of summer to your table year-round. This simple pasta salad shows them off at their best.

> 2 tablespoons lemon juice
> 1 tablespoon balsamic vinegar
> 1 teaspoon creamy Dijon mustard
> ¼ teaspoon sugar
> 2 medium garlic cloves, finely chopped
> Salt and pepper
> 1 tablespoon olive oil
> 1¾ pounds firm ripe Roma tomatoes, halved, stemmed,
>   seeded (see page 8), and coarsely chopped
> 1 tablespoon finely shredded fresh basil leaves
> 1 tablespoon finely chopped fresh chives
> 1 tablespoon finely chopped fresh Italian parsley
> ¾ pound farfalle, ruote, or other medium-sized pasta shapes

In a mixing bowl, stir together the lemon juice, balsamic vinegar, mustard, sugar, garlic, and salt and pepper to taste. Stirring briskly, pour in the olive oil. Add the tomatoes, basil, chives, and parsley and toss well. Taste and adjust the seasoning, then cover and refrigerate.

Bring a large pot of water to a boil. Add the pasta and cook until al dente, following manufacturer's suggested cooking time. Drain well. Rinse under cold running water, then drain well again.

Toss together the pasta and tomato mixture and refrigerate until serving time.

Serves 4

NUTRITIONAL ANALYSIS PER SERVING
Calories: 391   *Total fat:* 5.33 g
Saturated fat: .73 g   *Cholesterol:* 0 mg
Sodium: 55 mg

Index